Praise for Stepl

"A very intelligent and highly skilled teacher of acting. Actors find him exciting to work with and get a great deal from his particular form of teaching."
—**John Houseman**, Academy Award, founding Director of the Drama Division/The Juilliard School

"I have been intrigued and impressed with Mr. Book's special abilities and with the progress immediately observable. I find his work most valuable."
—**Alan Schneider**, Tony award; the "most favored director" of Albee, Pinter, Beckett; former Director of the Drama Division/The Juilliard School

"I commend Stephen Book's work and highly recommend him to the theater community."
—**Viola Spolin**, author of *Improvisation for the Theater*

Book on Acting: Improvisation Technique for the Professional Actor in Film, Theater, & Television

"Stephen Book manages to articulate a technique that both allows the actor to be specific in silence and active and emotionally affective when speaking. He helps you tap into that endless well which is human."
—**Viola Davis**, Academy Award, Tony award, Prime Time Emmy Award, Screen Actors Guild Award

"Improvisation is essential to acting and Book is a terrific teacher."
—**William Hurt**, Academy Award

"In adapting improvisation exercises to script work, Stephen Book challenges some of the received wisdom of modern American training and offers a practical method for professional actors who want to learn how to infuse their work with spontaneity. Book's exercises demonstrate how much further you can go, imaginatively speaking, when acting."
—*Backstage*

The Actor Takes a Meeting

"Book so beautifully articulates the psychology behind the interview process that I heartily recommend his book to every actor I know—and to anyone else who interviews often but wonders why his or her success rate is so darn low."
—***Backstage***

"Stephen Book's interview technique is one of the most valuable tools for the actor. It is a 'how-to' for making an authentic connection. I vividly remember one of the best general meetings I had—It was easy and fun, and the time just flew by. As we were saying goodbye and I finally glanced at her resume, I saw that she had indeed studied with Stephen Book. I was not surprised."
—**Liz Dean**, Casting Director (*The Good Doctor*, *Major Crimes*, *Star Trek: Picard*)

"Until Stephen taught me how to take a meeting, I was always shooting myself in the foot. His technique has cleaned up all that self-destructive behavior and smoothed the way for making the transition from stand-up to acting and starring in a series. Now, I can be in a room with the most powerful people in show business and shine."
—**Christopher Titus** (*Titus*)

"If you are not happy with where your career is at, it might not be your talent; it might be your meeting skills. *The Actor Takes a Meeting* is the first complete and comprehensive guide to insure a successful meeting. Bravo!"
—**Mary Goldberg**, Manager, former Casting Director for New York Shakespeare Festival/Public Theater

"As someone who has worked on both sides of the business, I can tell you firsthand that Stephen Book gets it exactly right. If you want to walk into a meeting or an audition with the kinds of tools and knowledge that give you the confidence to be your absolute best, *The Actor Takes a Meeting* is a book you should study and enjoy."
—**Grant Heslov**, Academy Award, Producer (*Argo*)

"As a former agent, manager, and producer I've taken countless meetings with actors who desperately needed this advice. He even paints a clear picture of how I've been reacting to what you've been doing wrong. I had no idea it was that transparent."
—**Bruce Smith**, President, OmniPop Talent Group

"*The Actor Takes a Meeting* is a guide to changing the actor's fear into authenticity and presence. This book is a gift to the actor."
—**April Webster**, Prime Time Emmy Award, Casting Director (*Criminal Minds*, *Lost*, *Star Trek*)

Stephen's Workshops

"Stephen's class is wonderful! You come away feeling that you have secret magic stuff to add to what you already know about acting."
—**Valerie Mahaffey**, Prime Time Emmy Award

"Stephen Book's Improvisation Technique is creatively explosive! It has heightened my presence with new levels of freedom, authenticity, and generosity. Right after completing Stephen's class, I booked *Buffy* which led to *Angel*, *Bones*, and films."
—**David Boreanaz**

"Prior to Stephen's class, I often felt I was flying by the seat of my pants, but his workshop has given me invaluable tools that I can use forever. He's the man!"
—**Malcolm-Jamal Warner**

"The training gave me a brand-new perspective on my work. It allows you to keep the techniques that you already know and use as a point of departure! It turns acting into 'play' again. Stephen Book is wonderful!"
—**Tim Matheson**

"From the first rehearsal to the last take, his work is invaluable. It helps you to get out of your own way and gives you a feeling of doing improv while using text. He's a great coach. Don't do a film without him!"
—**Tate Donovan**, Prime Time Emmy Award, Screen Actors Guild Award

"Working with Stephen helps keep my work fresh, colorful, and interesting. When I'm on the set, I feel more and more prepared, and at the same time, ready for anything. Stephen contributed immeasurably to my receiving two Emmy nominations in 1986."
—**Peggy McCay**, Prime Time Emmy Award, two Daytime Emmy Awards

"Stephen Book's Improvisation Technique has made me a better actor and a better stand-up—both in performance and writing. I've learned how to think and do bigger and better."
—**Adam Ferrara**

"I learned how to improvise (with confidence!), and to use it as a tool in performance—without changing one line of script! It's no coincidence that one year after joining Stephen's workshop I won an Emmy."
—**Leann Hunley**, Daytime Emmy award

"I strongly recommend Stephen's workshop. It gave me a new sense of freedom and spontaneity in my work and helped me to break those old and stale habits."
—**Veronica Cartwright,** Prime Time Emmy Award

"Thelonious Monk once said, 'The only cats worth anything are the cats who take chances. Sometimes I play a song I never even heard.' In a song or in a scene, Stephen Book's technique will lead you to take that kind of chance. You will sing a song you've never even heard."
—**Jack Riley**

"Simply put, Stephen's Improvisation Technique workshop transformed my craft and career. From breaking down a script to all the invaluable tools that address every need of the working actor, his technique has helped me create fuller characters, make better acting choices, and raise immeasurably the quality of my work."
—**Anna Khaja**

"Book is truly a master teacher. He is the only teacher I ever worked with who teaches pure technique—tools for handling every situation, problem, and role."
—**Larry Drake**, Two Prime Time Emmy Awards

Secret MAGIC STUFF FOR ACTORS

Also by Stephen Book

Book on Acting: Improvisation Technique for the Professional Actor in Film, Theater & Television

The Actor Takes a Meeting: How to Interview Successfully with Agents, Managers, Producers, and Casting Directors

Secret MAGIC STUFF FOR ACTORS

★||||| SOLUTIONS FOR ALMOST EVERY SITUATION |||||★

Stephen Book

SILMAN-JAMES PRESS   LOS ANGELES

Copyright © 2025 by Stephen Book

All rights reserved. No part of this book may be used or reproduced in any manner whatsoever without written permission from the publisher, except in the case of brief quotations embodied in critical articles and reviews.

First Edition

10 9 8 7 6 5 4 3 2 1

978-1-935247-33-3

Cover design by Wade Lageose for Lageose Design
Author photo by Kevin Langdon Ackerman

Printed and bound in the United States of America

Silman-James Press
www.silmanjamespress.com

To Pippa and Ries for inspiration and for the future.

CONTENTS

Preface *xv*

SPECIAL STUFF *1*

I   QUESTION AND ANSWER RAILROAD TRACKS *3*
Discovering your character's private thoughts leads to spontaneous and improvisational thinking *as* the character instead of *for* the character.

II   ATTITUDE LINES: PROCESS AND ARCHETYPES *9*
Possessing the character's core attitude provides the character's physicality, personality, and essence.

III   REFLECTION LISTENING *27*
Listening with the whole body heightens authenticity, spontaneity, and presence.

IV   PHYSICALIZING AN EMOTION *31*
The wordless conversation between the body and the mind creates the desired emotion with countless possibilities that exist within that feeling.

V   EMOTION ARC *51*
Increasing the intensity of an emotion over the length of a speech, beat, monologue, or scene is forceful and compelling.

VI   UMBRELLA ARC *57*
Shaping your character's emotional journey leads to more powerful scenes.

VII   MONOLOGUES: BREAKDOWN AND REHEARSAL *67*
Revealing something about the character that is not mentioned in the monologue intensifies the monologue's emotional impact.

ALL THE STUFF 77

VIII DOING 79

WHEN YOU NEED TO:

Play Drunk *81*

Play Stoned *84*

Pick Up the Pace *85*

Do a Walk-and-Talk *88*

Seduce Another Character *90*

Think on Camera or Stage *93*

Play the Story *97*

Play the Subtext *100*

Make a Monologue Compelling *110*

Make the Exposition Compelling *116*

Do It Again Just Like That *122*

Do a Contradictory or Contrasting Direction *125*

Do the Director's Line Reading *126*

IX EMOTIONS *129*

WHEN YOU NEED TO:

Play a Specific Emotion *131*

Make a Sharp Transition from One Emotion to Another *141*

Intensify an Emotion Instead of Flatlining *147*

Cry *152*

Laugh *179*

Leave your Acted Emotions Behind and Go On to the Next Scenc or Go Home *182*

Deal with Being Nervous *183*

X CHARACTER *189*

WHEN YOU NEED TO:

Quickly Change to the Director's Vision of the Character *191*

Make the Character More Physically Distinctive *194*

Make It More Quirky *199*

Change your Relationship Status *202*

Make a Decision About What Your Character Knows *208*
Get the Role on Track *210*

XI LESS IS MORE *213*

WHEN YOU NEED TO:

Take It Down *215*
Tone It Down *217*
Relax and Simplify *219*
Just Talk and Listen *221*
Stop Acting! *222*
Just be Yourself — No Character! *223*

XII MORE IS MORE *225*

WHEN YOU NEED TO:

Be in the Middle of the Scene when "Action" is Called *227*
Do a Pre-Scene Improv *229*
Give It More Energy *239*
Fill That Pause *241*
Commit to the Moment *244*
Nail a Close-Up (Listening) *246*
Listen to a Monologue in a Compelling Fashion *250*
Nail a Close-up (Speaking) *251*

XIII CAREER *257*

WHEN YOU NEED TO:

Improve Your Self-Tapes *259*
Accept or Reject a Job *264*
Increase Your Opportunities *266*

Appendix A Sample Umbrella Arcs *267*
Appendix B Sample Character Arcs *271*
Appendix C Sample Emotion and Attitude Choices *272*
Appendix D Sample Attitude Lines *274*
Appendix E Sample Action (Verbs) Choices *276*
Acknowledgments *279*
About the Author *280*

PREFACE

Your job is to show up on time, know the text and have a head full of ideas.
—Tom Hanks

You prepare your ass off and then when you're ready to shoot, you throw it all away and see what has stuck.
—Mike Nichols

Not far from Times Square in New York City is the Actors Studio. It was a fall evening in 1975 and the Directors Unit session had just ended. I was coming down the stairs from the theater workspace to the reception area and Shelley Winters was waiting for me at the bottom. I was surprised and concerned when she said, "Stephen, can we see you in Lee's office for a few minutes?" Joining us in the office were David Garfield and another actor whose name is lost in my memory. Shelley explained to me they were a committee designated to solve a problem around Lee Strasberg's frequent absences from the studio sessions. Lee was now spending lots of time in Los Angeles due to his newfound success as a film actor since *The Godfather II,* and the opening of his privately owned Lee Strasberg Institute in West Hollywood. Until now they had relied on the usual substitute moderators: Arthur Penn, Shelley, Estelle Parsons, Mel Shapiro, and others who happened to be in town to fill in at the last minute. She pointed out that this process had become too unwieldy and it had been decided to appoint a permanent substitute to cover all the sessions Lee couldn't attend. Would I accept the position?

I was stopped cold with the significance of this invitation. I was thirty years old and recently married, had come back to NYC five years earlier to start my directing career, and discovered I wouldn't have to wait tables between gigs because I was pulling down gigs as an acting teacher. After no more than ten seconds, during which I mused on the concept of being the Actors Studio's choice as Lee Strasberg's permanent substitute, I told them how pleased I was to be asked, but "No." I told them that, between my directing career and teaching my classes at Juilliard, I couldn't make that kind of additional time commitment.

That was true, but not the real reason. At the time, I was developing an acting technique that was antithetical to Lee's and the studio's method. I knew if I took the gig, it wouldn't take long for the members to start a revolution against me. Actors frequently feel like they know all they need to know about acting technique. Unfortunately, this is more like the blind man and the elephant. Every part you touch fools you into thinking you know the whole thing. But I don't think anyone can really know everything about acting technique. It's too big, too personal, and too mysterious. My overall approach to actor training includes character development and emotional work not dependent on any examination of the self or on playing an action that brings emotion with it. It provides the actor with the ability to instantly create any emotion on demand with no preparation time. I believe a director should be able to say to an actor, "You need to be (any emotion or attitude choice)." The proficient actor then provides it, and they see if the choice works. Many of the folks at the Actors Studio and many actors who follow their method would denigrate any such direction and sneer that that's a "result" direction. Some actors are not prepared to do something an actor should be able to do, and they blame their inability on the director giving the wrong kind of notes. If I had moderated sessions at the Studio without having the opportunity to first train the actors to be able to do my suggestions in the character and emotional areas, every session would have disintegrated into debates and arguments. In that moment, when Shelley extended the invitation, a Japanese expression came to mind with new significance: The hawk with talent hides its talons.

The technique I was developing would eventually become Improvisation Technique, an expansion of Spolin Theater Games into a scripted acting technique for the individual actor. I wrote the training manual for it in 2002, *Book on Acting: Improvisation Technique for the Professional Actor in Film, Theater & Television* (Silman-James Press). In 650 pages devoted to a complete acting technique, important features and tools ended up submerged. Directing and coaching actors who were not my students, I discovered key elements were valuable on their own and could be separated out from the entire Improvisation Technique. I decided to write *Secret Magic Stuff for Actors* in order to share the goodies I have seen my students and clients rely on. They delight in sharing stories about how pleased directors are when they respond to directions with immediacy, conviction, and facility—"You want me to cry here? Sure, no problem. Let's do it. I'm ready." My book's title comes from a blurb Valerie Mahaffey gave me: "Stephen's class is wonderful! You come away feeling that you have secret magic stuff to add to what you already know about acting."

If you are an actor who is new to the game and are only beginning to develop a personal technique, you may frequently feel stymied by certain directors' notes. If you are a veteran actor, sometimes, regardless of the overall effectiveness of your personal technique or your command of it, you just can't figure out what to do that will fulfill the director's note or get you where you need to be in the script. Maybe your commitment to the pursuit of an objective or being in the moment isn't enough for the situation.

When your personal technique isn't enough, you have an opportunity to think outside the box. Thinking and doing outside the box is one of the ways we grow and evolve as humans and as professionals. Elia Kazan and Mike Nichols, two of America's greatest directors in both film and theater, were also considered top actors' directors and are referred to throughout the book, along with insights from multiple well-known actors. Kazan said, "There simply aren't any absolutes... to find the way to make happen what you want to have happen on screen or on stage. You have to do whatever the hell it takes to get for yourself what you are after. ...There is no single way to do it. You must never be afraid to try anything you feel might help."

This book provides tools you can take to the set or rehearsal and use to solve problems that your basic technique cannot. You'll find approaches here that you may not know about—secret magic stuff!

The book is divided into sections for ease in locating the appropriate tool. Each section covers a different aspect of acting technique with a list of specific situations you may encounter, followed by one or more solutions for each situation. Many of the solutions involve the Secret Magic Stuff I have developed over the years and find to be most effective with the quickest results. Those solutions that involve the Secret Magic Stuff are highlighted by a star ★. You will also find more traditionally oriented solutions, some with secret magic variations, for the actor familiar with and preferring traditional technique (intentions, objectives, actions, etc.). Beginners will profit from considering all the solutions and developing an understanding of different approaches to solving the same acting problem.

This book assumes that readers have basic acting skills and their own approach to creating a character and playing it with conviction. They know the fundamentals of given circumstances—how the undisputed details of the script's world (place, time, characters, and events) influence all acting choices. Some of the more traditional solutions also assume the actor has the skill of playing an action—what you do from moment to moment to get what you want. If you do not already have this important skill, there are plenty of books and classes devoted to playing actions and working from within the Stanislavsky heritage. While it's hard to imagine an actor who hasn't learned the principle that an actor must know what her character wants, Cate Blanchett supports another point of view: "I don't have to answer that question. Because by answering that question, I'm pinning it down. Trying to pin the character down and say: That's who she is. That's what she's after. Because we're not like that." Many secret magic solutions bypass this issue and show you other approaches. If you employ a traditional technique based on objectives and actions to arrive at your choices and the spontaneous playing of them, then the secret magic stuff can be additional tools available to you for further exploration should you choose to sacrifice the security of what you know for the thrill of adventure and discovery. The solutions do not rely on a single technique. When a solution includes the use of an acting tool not well known, I provide a more thorough explanation. For example, in the entries about emotions, some of the alternative solutions tell you to physicalize an emotion, and I have provided a few exercises to help you to learn this tool. In particular, there are seven secret magic tools that come in handy for various solutions and will probably be considered "outside the box" by many actors. These tools and their learning exercises are found in the section Special Stuff.

In any single entry, I encourage you to peruse all the solutions in order to see the big picture. You can then decide which solution appeals to you. Be open to tools you haven't found in your personal technique. In TV and film, there's very little time for rehearsing with cast mates and the director. Even just reading the solutions may open doors or inspire your own creativity in solving problems, either with planning and rehearsal or in the moment.

My goal is to provide exciting solutions for stage or camera for what to do in particular situations. Employing these solutions will extend your abilities and heighten your confidence. Acting with confidence instantly raises your game to a different level. My solutions are tested and drawn from over fifty years of experience as a student, actor, director, teacher, and coach. In that time, I have also learned from all my students and all the actors I have coached or directed. My students have included William Hurt, Rita Moreno, Robin Williams, Val Kilmer, Sanaa Lathan, George Carlin, Maura Tierney, David Boreanaz, Carla Gugino, Malcolm-Jamal Warner, Valerie Mahaffey, and Tim Matheson.

Since this is not an academic book, I seldom describe the evolution of my solutions or trace them to who or what led me to them. I have worked in a variety of ways with Viola Spolin, Lee Strasberg, Gerald Hiken, Susana Bloch, John Houseman, and Alan Schneider. I must register the influence, direct or indirect, of Konstantine Stanislavsky, Michael Chekhov, Richard Boleslavski, Bobby Lewis, Stella Adler, Uta Hagen, Sandy Meisner, Keith Johnstone, and Mike Nichols. By the time I came to write this book, my solutions therefore were the product of instinctive interpretation, invention, modification, and problem solving.

I always find comparisons between actors and dancers to be illuminating. They are both performing artists with the same instrument—the body. One difference is that, when dancers are introduced to new steps or a combination, they discover in the very act of doing it all they need to know about it—where it works or doesn't, what needs fine tuning, etc. When some actors are given a suggestion, they too often ruminate, ponder, analyze, or question the suggestion, instead of just doing it and seeing what happens. This deprives them of the spontaneity of discovery. The tools in the actor's toolbox, like all tools, are best used after a little practice. The body will learn how the tool works and how to use it within the spontaneity of being in the moment. Practice can improve your performance, perhaps far more than you imagined.

SPECIAL STUFF

*It should be possible to reconsider
the efficiency of the wheel.*
—Edward De Bono

I knew there was more going on than they were telling us.
—Jerry Garcia

[top]: Stephen Book (Creative Consultant) directs the supporting cast to use **Question and Answer Railroad Tracks** on the set of *What Dreams May Come*.

[bottom]: Vincent Ward (Director) and Stephen Book on the set.

QUESTION AND ANSWER RAILROAD TRACKS

The distinguished actor Michael Caine has won two Academy Awards and been nominated six times. He says, "A film actor must be sufficiently in charge of his material and in tune with the life of his character to think his character's most private thoughts as though no one were watching him—no camera spying on him. The camera just happens to be there."

Question and Answer Railroad Tracks is a tool for achieving your character's spontaneous and improvisational thinking of private thoughts. It enables the actor to think *as* the character, not as an actor *for* the character. The audience will not know what you are thinking, but they will know your character is thinking real thoughts. The character is frequently seen thinking while listening to another character, such as during a lengthy monologue, or in a close-up or medium close-up reaction to something seen or heard. Viola Davis told me she used Question and Answer Railroad Tracks to maintain spontaneity listening to Denzel Washington's monologues in *Fences*, eight performances a week on Broadway. She won the Tony for her performance and then the Oscar for the movie.

To start: The question

When your character needs to be seen thinking, improvise a single question in your mind about whatever your character is supposed to be thinking about—for example, "What do I do now?" Any question will do. If you don't know what your character is supposed to be thinking about, start off listening to the other character, your scene partner, in your usual way and stay alert to something the other character says that can provoke a secret question in your mind. Here are some examples: "Why did he say that?," "How would he know that?," "What does he want from me?," or "How can I get away from him?" It bears repeating that any question will do.

Next: The answer

Answer the question in your mind. Make up an answer based on whatever your character knows or doesn't know at this moment in the script. Don't be concerned with searching for the best or correct answer. No one will ever know what you come up with. It's just for you. Here are some examples: "What do I do now? I have to go to somewhere safe."; "Why did he say that? He is trying to impress me."; "What does he want from me? He wants money."; "How can I get away from him? I'll tell him I don't feel well."

Next: Another question

After coming up with your answer, let the answer point you to a second question you improvise to yourself. Here are some examples: "I have to go to somewhere safe. Should I go home or to my friend's house?"; "He is trying to impress me. Why would he need to impress me?"; "He wants money. Do I want to give it to him?"; "I'll tell him I don't feel well. Will he believe me?"

1 QUESTION AND ANSWER RAILROAD TRACKS 5

Next: An answer to the second question

Improvise an answer to this second question. Here are some examples: "Should I go home or to my friend's house? My friend's house is safer."; "Why would he need to impress me? He wants me to like him."; "Do I want to give money to him? No."; "Will he believe I am not feeling well? I don't know."

Next: A third question

After coming up with your answer, let it point you to a third question you improvise to yourself. Here are some examples: "My friend's house is safer. Will I put her in jeopardy?"; "He wants me to like him. Should I let him know that I do like him?"; "No, I do not want to give him money. How's he going to react?"; "I don't know if he'll believe I'm not feeling well. What if I tell him I have a business appointment?"

Next: An answer to the third question

Improvise an answer to this question. Then keep going (question → answer → question → answer) for as long as you need to be seen listening and thinking.

This tool is called Question and Answer Railroad Tracks because it provides the means for traveling further through the scene and through the character's thoughts. Each question and each answer is another tie along the track. Before you know it, you are traveling through these questions and answers, and you just keep going, traveling in a purposeful manner towards an unknown destination. Just do the thinking for real. Don't muscle anything to make sure the camera sees it. If you're doing a close-up, so long as you don't go out of your way to freeze your face muscles, your natural face and eyes will reveal there is something going on. What makes this compelling to watch is that you are actively doing something in addition to appearing to be listening; there is something else going on in your mind. You will also discover how your character thinks and what they are thinking about with only a few improvised questions and answers. Traveling on the railroad tracks not only has you thinking in character, it shows you who you are.

All questions and answers are improvised in the moment. For multiple takes or performances, to guarantee spontaneity, improvise a new first question every time. You may also choose at any time to get off the tracks and fully listen (attentively) to the speaker while waiting for an opportunity to select a new secret question and start a new set of Question and Answer Railroad Tracks.

Railroad Track Turns

Especially useful in your close-up reaction shot, and to give the director an opportunity to stay on you longer than he anticipated, create a *turn*—leaving one set of railroad tracks for another set going in a different direction. If the turn is wide enough, it should produce a change of attitude or emotion. The turn may be accomplished by a topic change in your questions and answers if it creates a new insight, attitude, or emotion. The turn is completed when you have started questions and answers on a completely different track from the previous set of questions and answers. Every time you take a turn, the camera, director, editor, and audience see the turn and are drawn to it. They want to know what just happened. What caused you to change your attitude, emotion, or demeanor? Without turns, the audience gets used to the direction you are going in. The editor knows that this feeling in the audience is his enemy and will cut away from you and look for the action somewhere else. The more turns you make, the more interesting the trip will be for you and for the audience. Turns are most effective when there is greater distance between the two sets of tracks, in other words, a wide turn. Your acting, the thinking, becomes more dynamic and less likely to be cut in the editing room. This is also true when you provide multiple turns. Assume that the editor will cut away from you if you go more than three questions and answers on a railroad track without a turn.

Here is an example of a turn occurring after three questions and answers on a single railroad track. My character and his girlfriend are at a party, and she has a monologue that builds to her breaking up with me. I'm listening to her and at the same time traveling on a railroad track. Is she going to leave me? Yes. Why? She's found someone else. How do I feel about this? I need a drink. Do I want to deal with that crowd at the bar? With that last question, I make the turn and am now on a new track. This turn is closely related to the track I've just turned from, but it doesn't have to be. The turn is improvised. Every situation is different. Your character, the dialogue, and the given circumstances will guide you and keep you within the parameters of the scene.

When you start to feel comfortable with the railroad track you are on, take that as a cue to make a turn and get on another track. One question that can be introduced at any point on any set of railroad tracks and will usually provoke a turn is: "Do I want to tell him (your scene partner) what I'm thinking?" Answer this question and continue down this track until your next turn. If you feel the need to highlight a turn, change the focal point of your eyes (not moving your whole head, but only your eyes to the left or right or up or down) at the moment of the turn. This tool should only be used sparingly as it is a crutch and can make turns appear heavy-handed with frequent usage. Use it for takes where your eye-line is a taped X to the side of the camera and the speaker is behind the camera.

On *What Dreams May Come,* starring Robin Williams and Cuba Gooding Jr., I was creative consultant to the director, Vincent Ward. In the editing room, I saw that, if an actor stayed in the same reaction, they cut away. But every time the reaction shot of the actor had just a slight turn, they kept it. They didn't even bother to discuss what the change represented. The turn hooks the audience; they want to know what happened. The editors and directors keep the turns because they're where the movement is. The turn is the action in the reaction.

> You will find Question and Answer Railroad Tracks suggested as a tool in some of the solutions in the entries **Play the Subtext,** p.100; **Think on Camera**, p. 93; **Nail a Close-Up, Solution #2— Listening While Thinking About Other Things**, p. 246; **Improve Your Self-Tapes**, p. 259.

ATTITUDE LINES: PROCESS AND ARCHETYPES

It's very important to script writers that their characters are consistent. You will find one specific and consistent core attitude underlying everything a character says and does. It affects how they hold their body, walk, talk, and relate to other characters. When you possess and embody that core attitude, you will also create the character's personality and spontaneously think and feel as the character.

Whether you are creating a character from scratch or changing your characterization due to a director's feedback, an important tool is the **Attitude Line**. An attitude line is a personal expression of the character's core attitude, worded as succinctly and directly as possible. Here are some examples: I'm enthusiastic; I'm insecure; I'm the best; Nobody loves me; I'm sweet; I'm lonely; I'm mean; I love life; I'm pretty; I'm smart; I'm the smartest; I'm happy; I'll try anything; I'm impatient; I'm worth it; I'm shameless; I know best.

Look at the text to find the clues to the character's core attitude. *What single attitude is consistently shown in most of the character's lines?* It might be a consistent point of view—for example, the character is always expressing opinions (I know best); is mean to everyone (I'm mean); is always making jokes (I'm funny); is always insisting on people doing things her way (I'm in charge). Sometimes, writers construct their scripts around a character's attitude being thwarted by the story or other characters, which makes for drama or comedy. Sometimes, the character will actually say his attitude line in the dialogue and even repeat it. When that happens, the writer is making sure the audience (and you) gets it. It's on you, the actor, and the interpretive artist, to discern from the script the character's attitude and then turn it into an attitude line. Once you think you have it, hold it up to every line your character says and check that it is suitable for most of the lines. Also check it against the writer's character description in the script, any director's comments, the casting director's cast breakdown description, what the character reveals about himself, and what other characters say about him. Don't fool yourself into minimizing the casting director's breakdown. The first draft of that breakdown description is written by the folks at Breakdown Services and then reviewed and rewritten by the casting director, followed by the director, producer, studio, and sometimes (but not always) the writer.

For further clarification on picking out the clues to the attitude line, let's use as an example Amanda in *The Glass Menagerie*. Her attitude line would be either *I know best* or *I'm in charge*. An actor working on creating Amanda's character would be wise to separately explore both attitude lines and ultimately select the one she prefers. From Amanda's point of view, she knows best. Based on the number of orders she gives, we must also consider *I'm in charge*. Either attitude line will provide much of the play's drama, as she is frequently opinionated, demanding, and thwarted in her desires. Her daughter, Laura, says to her, "Mother, when you're disappointed, you get that awful suffering look on your face..." For our purposes, there are too many clues pointing to either attitude line to list all of them, so here are some of the clues that represent these attitudes from each of the play's seven scenes. After reading these clues, you should understand how to spot other clues.

You could select *I know best* based on her constant opinions stated as facts. The clues for selecting *I'm in charge* are the orders or authoritative commands she makes to her children.

Scene 1: [*I'm in charge*] "Honey, don't push with your fingers. If you have to push with something, the thing to push with is a crust of bread." [*I know best*] "A well-cooked meal has lots of delicate flavors that have to be held in the mouth for appreciation." [*I'm in charge*] "So chew your food and give your salivary glands a chance to function!"

Scene 2: [*I know best*] "I know so well what becomes of unmarried women who aren't prepared to occupy a position." [*I know best*] "When people have some slight disadvantage like that, they cultivate other things to make up for it—develop charm—and vivacity—and—*charm*!" [*I'm in charge*] "That's all you have to do."

Scene 3: [*I know best*] "It's the *Gone with the Wind* of the post-World War generation!" [*I know best*] "I took that horrible novel back to the library—yes! That hideous book by that insane Mr. Lawrence."

Scene 4: [*I'm in charge*] "Rise and shine! Rise and shine! Laura, go tell your brother to rise and shine!" *[I know best]* "If anyone breaks a leg on those fire-escape steps, the landlord ought to be sued for every cent he possesses!" [*I'm in charge* and *I know best*] "Try and you will SUCCEED!" [*I know best*] "Most young men find adventure in their careers. They do or they do without it!" [*I'm in charge* and *I know best*] "Don't quote instinct to me! Instinct is something that people have got away from! It belongs to animals! Christian adults don't want it!" [*I'm in charge*] "We have to be making plans and provisions for her." [*I know best*] "What kind of life is that for a girl to lead?"

Scene 5: [*I'm in charge*] "Comb your hair! You look so pretty when your hair is combed!" "We can't have a gentleman caller in a pig-sty!" [*I know best*] "Nothing offends people worse than broken engagements." "Sounds to me like a fairly responsible job, the sort of a job *you* would be in if you had more *get up*." "You are the only young man that I know of who ignores the fact that the future becomes the present, the present, the past, and the past turns into everlasting regret if you don't plan for it!" "Character is what to look for in a man."

Scene 6: [*I know best*] "All pretty girls are a trap, a pretty trap, and men expect them to be. This is the prettiest you will ever be!" "It's rare for a girl as sweet an' pretty as Laura to be domestic! But Laura is, thank heavens, not only pretty but also very domestic."

Scene 7: [*I know best*] "That shows you're romantic! But that's no excuse for Tom." [*I'm in charge*] "And how about you coaxing Sister to drink a little wine? I think it would be good for her!" [*I know best*] "It seems extremely peculiar that you wouldn't know your best friend was going to be married!"

There are many more clues of the same type throughout the script. It's the consistency of the same attitude throughout the script that determines the character's attitude.

In his memoir, *A Life in Parts*, Bryan Cranston talks about building a character on the foundation of having a core quality or essence for the character. When Bryan was the director and I was the creative consultant on a series pilot for Comedy Central, *Special Unit*, I worked directly with the actors and used attitude lines to create that "core quality or essence" for each of the cast regulars. The attitude is the essence.

After selecting your attitude line, you will need to embody it in order to create the character. Choosing an attitude alone, without allowing it to affect the body, is almost worthless. The attitude line must affect the body in order for it to be ingrained and for the actor's body to become the character's body. Achieving this transformation will also unlock the character's inner world and form the personality. Meryl Streep has pointed out, "An actor's only job is to enter the lives of people who are different from us and let you feel what that feels like." On another occasion, she said, "You can see what it's like to walk in another's shoes, to feel what it's like to be inside them, to see out of different eyes." In addition to your posture, walking, object handling, thinking, feeling, talking, listening, and relating to others, you will also find in the Attitude Line the character's rhythms, outer and inner. All parts of your body and personality will fall into their proper placement, a complete inside and a complete outside. The following process is based on a Spolin theater game preparation (Hold It!). You can do the process by reading the instructions to yourself as you do it. For better effect, have someone else read them out loud to you and respond to them. Just tell the friend to wait for a signal from you, like a head nod, before reading the next instruction.

Attitude Line Process

Sit down (with nothing on your lap). Sit up straight with your feet flat on the floor. Take five big breaths—not slowly, but not rushed—with your eyes open. Inhale and exhale through the mouth. Put emphasis on the inhale, which should take less than a second and be directed to the center of your chest, then relax your exhales, about two seconds each. Take five of these breaths. Look around the room and name, out loud, objects and colors ("The floor is gray. There is a silver lamp. That is a green wall.") Don't just say "gray, silver, green." Say a short, truthful sentence with the objects and colors for three to five items.

Observe your own natural breathing for about 30 seconds. Then silently say your Attitude Line to yourself. Keep repeating it to yourself, not rushed. *The line reading should capture the meaning of the line.* For example, "I'm impulsive" would not be said very slowly. It would be said crisply, with a high degree of energy. The line reading for "I'm sad" should have some sadness in it. Matching the tone of the line reading increases your commitment to the truthfulness of the attitude line. After you find the line reading you like, repeat it to yourself over and over, not rushed, to the exclusion of all other thoughts. Keep your eyes open.

Without urgency, keep repeating the line silently to yourself throughout the entire process. For about 30 seconds, simply get used to repeating the line, and then allow different parts or sections of your body to respond to the message of the attitude. Allow about 10 to 30 seconds for each section. As you respond with your body parts, actually *move that body part around until you feel it taking on the attitude and you have found the best positioning for expressing it.* When you find it, hold on to it. Start with the feet. Keep repeating the line to yourself, always with the line reading that captures the meaning of the line, and send the line as a message to your feet. Move your feet around until your feet take on the feeling of your attitude line. When you feel your feet are expressing it, hold on to that positioning. Go up to your legs without losing the feet. Move your legs around until your legs take on the feeling of your attitude line and are expressing it. Now go up to the midsection (pelvis, waist, and lower stomach). Move your midsection around until you feel it

11 ATTITUDE LINES

affected by the attitude line. Hold on to that. Now go to the chest. Keep repeating the line to yourself. Move your chest around until you feel it affected by the attitude line—until your chest is expressing that attitude. Hold on to that. Go to your shoulders. Do one shoulder at a time. You want the attitude to sit on each shoulder. Do the elbows, wrists, and fingers. Don't let go of the body parts that you have already visited. Go to your back. Move your spine around until you feel the attitude sitting on each vertebra. How does someone sit who has this attitude? Hold on to that. Go up to the neck, the top of your head, your eyebrows, the tip of your nose, your jaw, your lower lip. Add your tongue and your breathing. Allow your attitude to affect your breathing. Let your mouth and your breathing express the attitude. Make sure your face is expressing the attitude.

Increase the volume of your inner line-reading and send it to your whole body. Press your feet to the floor with that attitude. Stand up and walk around with the attitude and continue to have a whole-body response to your attitude line. You are now walking with the attitude. When it feels right, hold on to the walk. Own it. You'll know you have it when it feels organic to the whole body's response to the attitude line. Do some activities while silently repeating the attitude line to yourself and sending it to all parts of the body. You can get dressed, fill a plate at craft services, or do any of your character's stage business.

Engage with others (crew, cast, family, or friends), and discover how your new character talks and socializes. While engaging or chit-chatting, *never say your attitude line out loud*. Refresh frequently by silently saying your attitude line to yourself and allowing your body to respond and go with it—enjoy discovering and becoming the character. Don't be shy about engaging with others even if your character is shy or laid back or mean and nasty. If you are doing this process on a set, perhaps to effect a quick change of your characterization due to a director's feedback [see Quickly Change to the Director's Vision of the Character, p. 191], welcome interactions with the crew and cast. Mingle and chat with anyone. See what's happening at craft services. Consider a snack and discover what snacks appeal to you or don't, and how you eat. Go with it. Go out there as the character and experience the character's life (if you are alone working at home, go out to a store in character and converse with salespeople). You may find some edges that need smoothing out or finishing. This is where the experience of acting is delicious. Playing the character is where the fun is. By now you will have experienced the transformative moment when an actor discovers and fully embodies the character. You have also discovered that you can improvise in character when mingling with others. You are now a whole character, in your character's body with a personality and total character specificity. Allow about 5 to 10 minutes for this section.

Go to the set in character and retain the body feeling of your attitude line. Keep your focus on holding on to this character and go with it. You can refresh it instantly by silently saying your line to yourself and allowing your body to respond. You should refresh whenever you feel the need to do so, even during a take or a performance. Always allow your body to respond when you refresh. Refreshing also serves as a trigger that can snap you back in character when you are having a bad day. It is also possible you will discover you don't need refreshers.

Play your acting choices and be open to changing the choices if they no longer fit. Or drop all previous acting choices and focus on retaining the attitude and character and just going with it.

While the attitude line readings to yourself are very important, stay open to the line reading changing over the course of the script. To experience what I mean, do the following quick exercise.

Say the attitude line **I know best** out loud. Say it a few times with different line readings and settle on a line reading you like for this attitude line. When you have the line reading you like, say the attitude line a few more times with that line reading to hold on to it.

Now, say it five more times and each time add an adjustment to it by using these adverbs:

(kindly) I know best
(cautiously) I know best
(adamantly) I know best
(warningly) I know best
(somberly) I know best

After saying the attitude line each of the above ways, you should understand immediately how the attitude line remains the same while your silent line readings to yourself when you refresh may alter as the script moves forward. However, when you refresh, you'll discover in the moment any necessary adjustments to the line reading. As the script advances, adjustments may also emerge when you may interpret a significant moment in the scene as a turning point for your character. An *attitude line reading switch* can highlight that moment and what follows, showing a change in the character's demeanor. Understanding these aspects of the attitude line is important when considering your choice of an attitude line and holding it up to your character's lines in the script to determine consistency and suitability.

When preparing his role of Walter White, the teacher-turned-drug dealer in the TV series *Breaking Bad*, Bryan Cranston's key to unlocking the character's essence was when he understood that the character was depressed and had given up. This discovery might have suggested "I give up" as an attitude line. But how would that work with the transformation the character goes through from a good guy to a bad guy over five seasons of the show? If "I give up" was the attitude line, the inner line reading would alter as the given circumstances of the story evolved. For instance, at the beginning, it would be a defeated line reading, as in "I give up (life has beaten me)." As the series progresses, the inner line reading changes and now reflects that he no longer feels defeated, and instead he feels challenged, as in, "I give up (but I'm not going to accept it)." As the series continues, the line reading changes and now reflects that he is powerful and challenging others, as in, "I give up (what are you going to do about it?)." By discovering new inner line readings when you refresh, you would portray the character's ongoing descent into corruption over five seasons while remaining consistent at his core. See for yourself by trying three different line readings for "I give up" and letting each one affect your body differently: (1) defeated, (2) challenged, (3) challenging others.

You will notice that your body's response to the line readings is: defeated-drooping; challenged-backing up; challenging-advancing. By the final season of *Breaking Bad*, on occasion, depending on what's happening in the story, Walter White sometimes flips back and forth between being challenged and challenging others.

In another example, let's say your character goes through a transformation near the end of the script, the attitude doesn't necessarily change. It might only be modified and expressed through a different attitude line line-reading. At the age of fourteen, a character whose attitude and personality expresses the belief that "nobody loves me" will feel desperate, alone, and maybe suicidal. That same character at the age of sixty-five will feel, perhaps, simply regretful, or even blasé, as if "nobody loves me (and what else is new?)." The character's attitude has not changed, only the given circumstances (in this case, advancing age). Research shows that most people get more calm, self-confident, and socially sensitive as they mature.

If you have difficulty figuring out the character's specific and consistent attitude line from the script or the director's comments, you might consider the tried-and-true archetypal attitude lines presented on the next two pages [p.20-21].

Keep in mind that it's the actor and not the character saying the attitude line to himself. Laurence Olivier, one of the greatest actors of the twentieth century, points out that in performance, "I am Othello... but Olivier is in charge." You create the character, and you—as the actor, not the character—refresh it when necessary by repeating the attitude line to yourself and making sure your body responds. Your inner refreshing of the attitude line is an actor's tool, and it will fuel the character's thinking and behavior.

Should your personal technique require that you find the humanity of the character in order to play him, you may feel challenged by some attitude lines. Let's take an extreme example to understand this point. Suppose you are playing a really evil villain, a pestilence, someone who doesn't care about right or wrong, only paths to his own benefit. All the clues in the script point to the attitude line "I'm evil." If you understand that this attitude line does not represent what the character thinks of himself, it allows space for the character to think of himself as humane—even if no one else would ever see him in this light. The attitude line enables you to play him as conceived by the writer and as you want others to see him—you want him to be seen as purely evil. Let's say, in order to find his humanity, you may justify his bad behavior as simply wanting to be more comfortable or needing more money or power. If you focus on his humanity, you might not capture the pure essence of this character—his evilness. Focusing on the character's

Attitude Lines for Archetypal Characters — MEN

White-collar professional — I'm confident; I know best

The good father — I know best; I know it all; I'm decent

Goofy friend — I'm enthusiastic; I mean well!; I'm funny

Innocent friend — I hope; I'm flexible; I'm compassionate; I'm sincere; I'm kind

Loyal friend — I'm steady; I'm in

Blue-collar everyman — I'm the boss; I'm great; I'm a nice guy

Blue-collar tough — I'm the boss

Villain — I'm in charge; I'm mean; I'm menacing; I'm dangerous; I'm in control

Bully — I want more; I'm mean; I'm better; I'm in charge

Rebel — I'm in charge; I know best

Leading man (charming) — I'm easy; I know best; I care; I have to; I'm silly

Gay coded man — I'm in control; I'm persistent; I'm fastidious; I'm discreet

Creepy, perverted jerk — I'm a winner; I'm frustrated

Teacher — I'm wise; I know best; I'm a teacher; I'm cautious

Tough, smart, strong, good — I'm relentless

Detective — I'm relentless

Snob — I'm important

Attitude Lines for Archetypal Characters — WOMEN

Good mother — I'm in charge; I know best; I have to; I care

Weak mother — I'm in charge; I know best (Note: She will always be thwarted.)

White-collar professional — I'm in control; I'm in charge; I know best; I have integrity

Leading lady — I know best; I have to; I'm fierce; I'm in control; I'm in charge; I'm thoughtful; I'm resourceful; I'm worth it

Leading lady (comedy) — I have plans; I know best; I'm entitled; I'm outrageous; I'm in charge; I know everything; I'm sarcastic; I'm impulsive

Leading lady (evil and powerful) — I want more; I want it all; I can do this; I'm in control; I'm in charge

Vixen (femme fatale) — I love men; I'm a flirt; I'm sexy

Dumb blonde — I'm impulsive; I'm spontaneous

Nuts — Heighten it!; I'm uncertain; I must!; I love life

Best friend or neighbor (comic relief) — I have plans; I know best; I'm entitled; I'm outrageous; I'm in charge; I know everything; I'm sarcastic; I'm impulsive

Blue-collar loser — I'm a rebel; I hate myself

Wife or Mom (comedy) — Why me?; I have plans; I know best; I'm entitled; I'm outrageous; I'm in charge; I know everything; I'm sarcastic; I'm impulsive

Tough, smart, strong, good — I'm determined; I'm fierce; I'm relentless; I know best

Detective — I'm relentless

Bitch — I'm entitled; I want more; I'm mean

Spinster — I care

humanity might deflect you from his way of behaving. According to Oscar Wilde, "Evil isn't what one does, it's something one is that infects everything that one does." If you feel the attitude line conflicts with finding the character's humanity, you will have to choose which approach you want to take. I recommend the attitude line. Don't worry about being liked. If you're playing a bad guy, make him bad. James Earl Jones, one of the few actors to have won the EGOT (Emmy, Grammy, Oscar, Tony), says that the job is "to strip ourselves of all sentimentality about what a human being is and to play that character as conceived by the author... to strip the character down naked to what he really is, with no apologies." Ray Liotta recalled his response to a review that said he played a sleazy, heartless, cold person who you don't really care about: "Great! I love it; that's what I played."

Attitude Lines and Sitcoms

In sitcoms, the characters' attitudes are dominant. The dean of sitcom directors, James Burrows (*Mary Tyler Moore*, *Taxi*, *Cheers*, *Friends*, *Frasier*, *Will & Grace*, and the pilots for *2½ Men* and *Big Bang Theory*) agrees: "One of the reasons *Friends* holds up is that there are six different ways of coming at things. You know what each character's attitude about everything is. If a subject is brought up, you know how each character will react. Every show I've done has that. *Taxi* and *Cheers* had seven. *Will & Grace* had four. You knew the issue and the attitude toward each issue. They're laughing at attitude. If you can get people to laugh at attitude and not a joke, you are home free."

If you have difficulty figuring out your character's specific and consistent attitude line from the script or the director's comments, you might consider the tried-and-true sitcom archetypal attitude lines on the following page.

Attitude Lines for Sitcom Archetypal Characters

(✓ Indicates my strong preference)

Logical smart one — ✓ I'm smart; I'm honest; I'm sarcastic; I'm reasonable

Lovable loser — ✓ I hope; I believe; I have faith; I'm hopeful; I'm impulsive; I'm optimistic; I'm determined; I have dreams

Neurotic — ✓ I must!; I'm obsessive; I'm controlling; I'm a neurotic!; I'm fussy; I analyze; I'm anxious; I'm insecure; I'm meticulous; I'm nervous; I'm a perfectionist

Dumb — ✓ I'm childlike; I'm confused; I'm sincere; I'm eager; I'm enthusiastic; I'm excited; I'm genuine; I'm supportive

Bitch — ✓ I'm condescending; I'm mean; I'm a bitch; I'm cynical; I'm tough; I'm sarcastic

Bastard — ✓ I'm mean (mischievous and biting line reading); I'm a bastard; I'm cynical; I'm tough; I'm sarcastic

Womanizer — ✓ I'm cocky; ✓ I love women; I'm smooth; I'm bold; I'm charming; I'm horny; I'm sexual

Manizer — ✓ I love men; I'm smooth; I'm confident; I'm bold; I'm charming; I'm horny; I'm sexual

Materialistic — ✓ I'm a princess; I'm proud; I impress; I'm a show-off; I'm the best; I'm above it all; I'm judgmental; I'm materialistic; I'm popular; I'm entitled; I'm shallow; I'm superficial

From another world (eccentric) — ✓ I'm odd; I'm spontaneous; I'm shameless; I'm fascinated; I'm optimistic; I'm positive; I'm ditzy

Conclusion

The magical prowess of an attitude line includes taking advantage of your unique self. As Julia Roberts says, "Because once you start the performance, that stuff that's inside us, that alchemy that makes us individuals, that's always going to bubble up to the surface in whatever way it needs to." Taking on an attitude line marries the written character, including his attitude, personality, behavior, and dialogue, to the uniqueness of the individual actor's response to having that attitude. This unique marriage of actor and character provides character specificity, transcends any generic expression of the attitude, and reflects that people experience emotions and attitudes differently. The attitude line "I'm sweet" does not mean that you will be sweet in every scene. You can still be angry, sad, or frightened when you need to be. At those times, we will get to see a character who has a sweet disposition get angry, sad, or frightened. The sweetness will be the character's essence and the core of the character's personality. An attitude line brings an easy fluidity to playing all the moments and acting choices. Even though the writer has chosen what you say and when you say it, the attitude will totally affect *how* you say the lines.

You can see attitude lines in operation if you view some of my students' film performances I have coached. Watch George Carlin, directed by Barbra Streisand and playing opposite her and Nick Nolte in *The Prince of Tides*. His attitude line is "I'm lonely." In the film *Memphis Belle,* Tate Donovan's attitude line, "I can do it," captured the writer's intent for the co-pilot playing second banana to the pilot and star, Matthew Modine. "I know best," a common attitude line for leading women, worked well for Sanaa Lathan when she played the lead in *Something New* and for Maura Tierney in *Instinct* as Anthony Hopkins' daughter.

See Appendix D for a lengthy list of sample Attitude Lines.

II ATTITUDE LINES

You will find Attitude Lines suggested as a tool in some of the solutions in the entries **Quickly Change to the Director's Vision of the Character**, p. 191; **Make the Character More Physically Distinctive**, p. 194; **Just Be Yourself. No Character!**, p. 222; **Commit to the Moment**, p. 244; **Do a Contradictory or Contrasting Direction**, p. 126.

Mars Callahan and Stephen Book in *Poolhall Junkies*. Stephen used **Reflection Listening** throughout this scene.

REFLECTION LISTENING

Reflection Listening creates authentic respect for the speaker and for what he is saying. It heightens authentic communication as you provide the speaker with your whole body in alertness and attention, without judgment, editorializing, commentary, or any form of inauthenticity.

Reflection Listening is not an appropriate acting tool when scenes are about a lack of communication—arguments, conflict, preoccupations, subtext, and emotional displays. It is appropriate when any aspect of the scene requires authentic communication and demands that the characters, at minimum, respect each other. It is an excellent tool for scenes about lovers. It can also be helpful in career interviews where you might tend to be nervous, inauthentic, or bored. You will be able to transcend these conditions and be present. Reflection Listening is a perfect tool for rehearsal or performance with stage or camera acting. Some of my students refer to the experience of Reflection Listening as "active listening." Spolin called her version Mirror Speech.

Reflection Listening is easily learned in a two-part exercise that takes less than 10 minutes.

Part 1: Have a conversation (2-5 minutes) with a friend or cast mate. Let the conversation flow back and forth between you. When your partner is speaking, mirror their lip movements with your own. Yes, your lips are moving silently as you repeat the same words your partner is saying with only a split-second lag between you. Hear the speaker's words, watch their lips, and move your lips, silently forming the same words. The only part of your body that is reflecting is your lips. When you are the speaker, you are not reflecting or doing anything special. After a few minutes, Reflection Listening should be easy to do. Let the conversation flow back and forth between you for a few more minutes and then stop.

Part 2: Resume the conversation. Do the same lip reflection process when your partner is speaking. Look at their lips in order to reflect them. Hear the speaker's words and silently repeat the same words to yourself. When you are about to move your own lips in reflection, don't move them. Don't misinterpret the last sentence—this is not just looking at their lips while listening. Your body should feel the same exact way it felt in Part 1. If it doesn't, you are not doing the exercise properly. One sign that you are not doing it properly will be if your mind wanders to other thoughts instead of silently repeating the speaker's words to yourself as she says them, even though you are no longer moving your lips. Keep your eyes on her lips as if you are going to move your lips in reflection. Do everything you did in Part 1 except for moving your own lips. You are playing Reflection Listening without letting an audience know you are doing it. You will know if your body feels the same as it did when you actually moved your own lips in Part 1. After a few minutes, Reflection Listening should be easy to do. You are ready to bring it to your performance.

In a camera close-up on you listening to the other character, do a take with Reflection Listening. Don't be concerned that it will look like you are looking at the other actor's lips. It doesn't, especially if there is at least two feet between you. It's your close-up, and you can ask your scene partner to step back a step or two if necessary. Besides, if it's your close-up, the audience can only see you and not what you are looking at.

In a shot that includes you and the character you are conversing with (for example, a two shot), the camera will see both you and your scene partner. Still, no one in the audience will think you are looking at the other's lips. See for yourself by watching an actor use Reflection Listening in a two shot in the film *Poolhall Junkies*, with Rod Steiger, Christopher Walken, and Chazz Palminteri. I was asked by the director, my friend Mars Callahan, to play the part of Laurence. Outside of demonstrations in my classes, I hadn't acted in over a decade. In my scene opposite Mars, who also played the lead, he is posing as a money manager, and I am seeking his advice. The scene is about a minute long and is captured in a single two shot with less than a foot between us. For the whole shot, I am completely focused on Reflection Listening. To anyone watching the film, it would never occur to them that I am looking at Mars' lips (and reflecting without moving my own lips). The scene occurs about 30 minutes into the film.

The Greek philosopher Galen said, "It's not the eyes that mirror the soul, it's the voice." Reflection Listening puts your focus on the speaker's voice and enhances and heightens your sincerity and respect while totally eliminating distraction and inauthenticity. You will find that the other's lips are so active compared to their eyes that your involvement in reflecting the activity of their lips takes you off of yourself and your (or your character's) hidden agendas, inner monologues, judgments, and future-tense thinking and planning. You're so busy doing something that you get out of your own way. The result is authentic communication between you and the other character in the moment, which only heightens the connection between what you see and hear and your responsive impulses. When you speak, you can look anywhere your impulse takes you. You will probably find that your impulse keeps you focused on their face in some fashion. Avoid using Reflection Listening when it's your scene partner's close-up. If he is not prepared for it, he may be thrown by the intensity of your listening.

For takes in which your eye-line is an X taped to the side of the camera and the speaker is behind the camera, you can't look at the speaker's lips and reflect their movements, but you can look at the X as if it was the speaker's lips and silently repeat their words in your mind. You'll feel empowered to hear the other's lines as if for the first time and your dialogue will be spontaneous and authentic.

In my experience, it is impossible to use Reflection Listening without having experientially learned it in Parts 1 and 2. In practice conversations, both conversation partners should play Reflection Listening (Parts 1 and 2). Don't regress to Part 1 and move your own lips! No one watching should know you are using Reflection Listening.

You will enjoy using Reflection Listening and will achieve a level of listening that is compelling to watch because it is full of your presence. You will be surprised by how much coverage is given to you in the final cut, even though a lot of it may be shots of you doing nothing but listening attentively.

You will find Reflection Listening suggested as a tool in some of the solutions in the entries **Do a Pre-Scene Improv**, p. 229; **Nail a Close-Up (Listening)**, p. 246; **Take It down**, p. 214; **Relax and Simplify**, p. 218; **Just Talk and Listen**, p. 220; **Just Be Yourself. No Character!**, p. 222.

IV

PHYSICALIZING AN EMOTION

Emotions occur when the body responds to a stimulus. The stimulus may come from within you, such as an idea, an anticipation, a desire, or a memory, or it may come from outside you, an external event. When you physicalize an emotion, you direct your body to take on the physical features and appearance associated with a specific emotion. The brain will recognize the changes in your body and activate the corresponding emotion. It knows that a particular emotion accompanies a particular physical pattern. Your body knows before the mind does, and there is a wordless conversation between the body and the mind. The body gives us a nudge, sending a signal to the brain in the form of, for example, a tensing or relaxing of the muscles, a shiver or a sigh, or a quickening of the breath. (Obviously, information flows in both directions, as you can think yourself into practically any emotional state and then have the face and body to match it, as in an Affective Memory.)

Visual artists experience this phenomenon when painting or drawing because the hand speaks to the brain as surely as the brain speaks to the hand. William James (considered the father of American psychology) proposed that emotions were the result, not the cause, of various bodily sensations, suggesting that "we feel sorry because we cry, angry because we strike, afraid because we tremble, and not that we cry, strike, or tremble, because we are sorry, angry, or fearful, as the case may be." As soon as you are aware of the stimulus, your body physically responds to it, followed by the feeling of the emotion. James' theory has been supported by multiple scientific studies addressing the relationship between physicalization and emotions, including a study in which depression was treated by paralyzing key facial muscles with Botox, which prevents patients from frowning and having unhappy-looking faces. Of the subjects who got Botox, 52% showed relief from depression, compared with only 15% who received the saline placebo. Another study found that posture doesn't just reflect our emotional states but can also cause them. One study shows that slouching while using your smartphone (called the iHunch, text neck, or iPosture) changes your mood, your memory, and even your behavior. When Robin Williams spoke of his training at Juilliard, he said he learned "There are certain gestures that are body language that are associated in your mind with an emotion."

While we were working on physicalization in a class, an actor commented:

"My little baby daughter, who's two, will sometimes pretend to be angry at something. She knows it's a way to manipulate. It's clear she's not really angry. She's only acting like she's angry, but as she does that, there comes a moment when she actually crosses over the line, unconsciously, into real anger."

This anecdote is an excellent illustration of physicalization. When the child acts like she's angry, she's physicalizing. She waves her hands, bangs the table, and does all the things that she does when she's angry. She physicalizes anger, which takes her into true anger.

Our feelings are strongly shaped by the way we hold and move our bodies. The more you physicalize the emotion in the acting state, the more quickly the emotion will come up. The process is vividly captured by the old aphorism "Do not wait to strike till the iron is hot; but make it hot by striking." When the body behaves as if it is feeling the emotion, the actual emotion emerges. Choose the emotion, physicalize it, and boom! The feeling is there and it comes naturally within the context of the scene. Physicalizing an emotion leads to a fresh experience of that emotion to match the new experience of the scene, rather than a retread of an old emotion (by way of memory) being applied to a new experience. If the feeling is not there—an occasional peril with any approach to acting emotions—at least you will look and act like you're experiencing the emotion and the audience or camera doesn't question it. That's called acting.

How to Physicalize an Emotion

Physicalization is learned experientially. Here are five progressive exercises. I recommend that you do the steps with a buddy, preferably an actor. Take turns doing the exercise while the other reads the directions out loud. If no one else is available, you can record the directions and play them back while you do the exercise.

Although you could do all the steps in one session, I recommend breaking them into two or three sessions. Any step is worth repeating for the sake of practice. If you do repeat a step, always change the emotion choice (unless you want practice with a particular emotion).

For most actors, this approach to emotions is entirely new. While going through the exercises, avoid using previously learned tools from your traditional technique. Physicalizing emotions prepares the actor for immediately playing a preselected emotion or fulfilling an emotion direction without a context of verbs, actions, problems, objectives, tasks, memories, visualizations, or as-ifs.

Step #1: Select an emotion from the Big Four—Anger, Happiness, Sadness, and Fear. The following directions should be spoken with a few seconds between each one; if you find that's too fast for you, ask your partner to slow down. Walk around as you respond to the directions. **Begin:** Focus on feeling the emotion with your toes. Physicalize it with your toes. If you chose happy, have happy toes. If you chose angry, have angry toes. Keep physicalizing it with your toes and add your whole feet. Choose to have your feet feel the emotion and move your feet around with the emotion—happy feet, angry feet, etc. As your feet express the emotion, add your knees. Physicalize the emotion with your knees. Then add the pelvic area. Feel the emotion with your pelvis. Physicalize it. The whole lower half of your body is now physicalizing the chosen emotion. If it helps you to feel it more, heighten the physicalization. Now, add your chest. You are now physicalizing the emotion with your chest. Keep physicalizing it, and add your shoulders. Move your shoulders around with the emotion. Add the elbows. If your emotion is sad, choose to have sad elbows. If it's anger, angry elbows, etc. Add the wrists [pause] the fingers [pause] your whole hands. Physicalize the emotion with your spine and feel it. Go up the neck. Move your neck around with the emotion. Add the top of your head [pause] eyebrows [pause] tongue [pause] eyes [pause] lower lip [pause] whole face. Use your whole body to physicalize the emotion. If you want to feel the emotion more, heighten the physicalization. Check if there are any parts of your body where you are not feeling or physicalizing the emotion. Keep physicalizing the emotion and heighten the physicalization in all your body parts. Observe your breathing. Sustain the physicalization of the emotion and bring down any exaggerated movements. Are you still exaggerating with your body? Do you still see remnants of the heightened body? You do not need any large, exaggerated movements. Stay focused on physicalizing the emotion. Check in with yourself and notice that you are feeling the emotion. Observe the feeling. Keep breathing. If you feel the

IV PHYSICALIZING AN EMOTION   35

emotion slipping, heighten the physicalization. If your response to the physicalization wasn't strong enough to make you feel the emotion, you just have to heighten the physicalization.

Before you take a break, lose the emotion by doing a **Step-Out**.

Step-Out

Pick a spot at eye level on a wall across the room. Look at that one spot and take five slow, long breaths, inhaling through the nose and exhaling through the mouth. Five counts to inhale. Five counts to exhale. Don't strain yourself. If you can't do five counts, do three or four. Look at that spot and do five inhales and five exhales. [Allow 1 minute]. When you finish the breaths, do some full body stretching and simultaneously speak gibberish out loud. Loudly. [Allow 1 minute]. With the fingertips of both hands, gently pat all over your face like you're playing the piano. Simultaneously, say to yourself, out loud in a very soothing voice, affirmations such as, "Hello, I love you. I love you. How is my old friend? Here we are together again. There are my lips. This is my nose. Here is my forehead. Hello." [Allow 30 seconds]. Now, bend over and pat your knees with your open hands. [Allow 10 seconds]. Like magic, emotional residue disappears.

You have just had an introductory taste of one of the two components in the process known as physicalizing an emotion. You selected an emotion, physicalized it, and arrived at feeling the emotion—all without employing any previously learned traditional or privately developed tools. You are beginning to develop a new tool for feeling and playing any emotion that requires only your choosing to physicalize it. As you practice the steps, you will decrease the amount of time between the moment you select the emotion and the physicalization and complete feeling of the emotion, eventually feeling it instantaneously.

Should a thought about the past or an image come to mind when you are physicalizing an emotion, that's all right. It arose spontaneously with the onset of the emotion. Avoid seizing on it and using it. Certainly, avoid going out of your way to create it. If it drifts in, allow it. Then allow it to drift out.

Step #2: Select an emotion from the Big Four, a different one from Step #1. The following directions should be spoken with a few seconds between sentences; if you find that's too fast for you, ask your partner to slow down. Walk around as you carry them out. **Begin:** Feel that emotion with your toes. Move your toes around in that emotion. Once you feel it there, keep it there as you then physicalize that emotion with your heel, your arch, and your whole foot. Move your feet around in that emotion. If your emotion is happy, what do happy feet feel like? What do sad feet feel like? Allow your feet to feel your selected emotion by physicalizing it. Keep it there and go up to the knees. Move your knees around in the emotion. Physicalize it with your knees. Heighten the movement if that helps you to feel it. It's up to you. You are physicalizing the chosen emotion with your feet and your knees. Move your pelvis around in that emotion. Now the whole lower half of your body is physicalizing the emotion. Add the chest. Don't lose the lower half of your body. Physicalize the emotion with your chest. Add the shoulders. Move your shoulders around in the emotion. If your selected emotion is happy, how do happy shoulders feel? How do sad shoulders feel? Allow your body to respond. Physicalize the emotion with your

IV PHYSICALIZING AN EMOTION

elbows...wrists...and fingers. Observe your spine physicalizing the emotion. If it isn't, physicalize the emotion with your spine. Physicalize it with your neck. There is lots of spine in the neck. Physicalize the emotion with your whole face. Include your eyebrows. What do happy eyebrows do? Angry eyebrows? Physicalize your emotion with your eyebrows. Go to your mouth and lips. What do a sad mouth and lips do? Happy mouth and lips? Physicalize your emotion with your mouth and lips. Your body will know what to do. Send the message and your body will do it. Allow your whole body to be in complete physicalization of this emotion. Keep physicalizing the emotion and at the same time bring down any large body movements to normal size. Without decreasing the physicalization of the emotion, take out any heightened or exaggerated body movements. Let's say we are shooting a movie right now, and you are in the scene. The set is a mall, and you are walking around the mall. Your job as an actor is to feel this emotion by physicalizing it, but the size of your body movements must be appropriate to someone walking in a mall. Observe your breathing. While you focus on walking and physicalizing the emotion, check in with yourself and observe if you are in fact feeling some degree of this particular emotion. Keep physicalizing it. [**Adding Objects**] You are no longer in the mall. Keep physicalizing the emotion and choose an activity to do with props—for example, cook a meal, apply makeup, get dressed, clean a room. Use real or invisible (space) props. While maintaining your body's physicalization of the emotion, imagine there is an audience and you want to show your emotion by how you handle the objects. It's as if all the audience can see is your arms, your hands, and the objects, and you want them to know how you feel. Feel what you are feeling and explore handling your props with that feeling. Every contact with a prop is an opportunity to show how you feel. Stay alert and take responsibility for every gesture. Every finger is an expression of the emotion: how you hold the prop, how you carry it, how you maneuver it, how you pull it, how you push it, how you adjust it, and, most importantly, how you use it. Every moment, be very aware of what your hands and arms are doing with the objects and showing how they feel [Allow 5-8 minutes for the preceding step]. End the activity and walk a little longer, continuing to physicalize the emotion. Observe your feelings. Notice if you have maintained, heightened, or lessened your feeling of the emotion since you began the activity. [Allow 30 seconds]. Cut.

Before taking a break, lose the emotion by doing a **Step-Out**.

Emotions that are felt but not communicated are of very little value. The second component of the physicalization process is the emotional handling of props or objects. How you handle your objects vividly shows an audience what you're feeling and, at the same time, heightens the feeling. You felt the emotion deepen as you focused on showing it through your object handling. It's like getting two for one: showing the feeling and increasing its supply.

Doing this exercise also heightens your awareness of the emotion while feeling it. With subsequent exercises and practice, this awareness expands into the will and control necessary for playing emotion arcs and switches.

Step #3: We will do this step, while walking around, with a few emotions. With each one, you will have less time to physicalize it. Allow about 5 seconds between sentences. Allow 20 second pause where indicated by [20 sec.].

SAD. Physicalize sad with your toes and heels. Have an immediate response. Go to the knees and move your knees around

IV   PHYSICALIZING AN EMOTION

in the emotion. Add the pelvis. Complete the physicalization throughout the lower half of your body. Add the chest, then the shoulders and elbows. If you need to heighten it in order to help yourself feel it, do so. Add the fingers, knuckles, and wrists. Every part of your body, from the neck down, is physicalizing sad. Add the face. Physicalize sad with your face. Heighten the whole body's physicalization. Are the parts of your body relaxed? Relax them more. Eyes slightly closed? Close them more and look through the eyelashes. Corners of the mouth pulling down? Pull them down further. Make sure that all parts of your body are physicalizing sad. Check in with yourself quickly and observe if you are feeling sad. Now, observe your breathing. [20 sec.] Lose sad. Shake it out as you walk. Take five long breaths, in through the nose and out through the mouth. [20 sec.] Speak gibberish out loud. [20 sec.] Walk around silently. [20 sec.] **JEALOUS.** Physicalize jealous with your toes and heels. Add the knees. Pelvis. Chest. Shoulders and elbows. Hands. Face. Heighten the entire physicalization. Check out your body parts. Anywhere you are not physicalizing jealous, do so now. Staying out of your head, quickly observe if you are feeling jealous. Now, observe your breathing. [20 sec.] Lose jealous. Shake it out as you walk. Take five long breaths, in through the nose and out through the mouth. [20 sec.] Speak gibberish out loud. [20 sec.] Walk around silently. [20 sec.] **SELFISH.** Physicalize selfish with the whole lower half of your body, from the waist to your toes. Physicalize selfish from the waist to the neck as well. You're now physicalizing selfish from your neck to your toes. Add your face. Physicalize a selfish face. You're now physicalizing selfish with your whole body. Check in with yourself quickly, and observe if you are feeling selfish. Stay out of your head and just quickly observe. Now, observe your breathing. [20 sec.] Lose selfish. Shake it out as you walk. Take five long breaths, in through the nose and out through the mouth. [20 sec.] Speak gibberish out loud. [20 sec.] Walk around silently. [20 sec.] **TENDER.** Physicalize tender with the whole lower half of your body. Add the upper half of your body, including your face. You're now physicalizing tender with your whole body. Check in with yourself quickly, and observe if you are feeling tender. Stay out of your head and just quickly observe. Now, observe your breathing. [20 sec.] Lose tender. Shake it out as you walk. Take five long breaths, in through the nose and out through the mouth. [20 sec.] Speak gibberish out loud. [20 sec.] Walk around silently. [20 sec.] **HAPPY.** Physicalize happy with the whole lower half of your body. Add the upper half of your body, including your face. You're now physicalizing happy with your whole body. Check in with yourself quickly, and observe if you are feeling happy. Stay out of your head and just quickly observe. Now, observe your breathing

Before taking a break, lose the emotion by doing a **Step-Out**.

You no longer have to go through all the separate body parts. By the last two emotions, the body parts were reduced to two groups, lower half and upper half. Your body is learning what to do and is recognizing what you want it to do more quickly.

Jealous and selfish may not have felt as authentic as tender and happy. They are not pure emotions and sometimes require a context, such as circumstances from a script. (How do you feel about your boyfriend looking at another woman? How do you feel about sharing audition information with a competitor?)

Step #4: We will do this step, while walking around, with a few emotions. With each one, you will have less time to physicalize it. Allow two seconds between sentences. Each [20 sec.] represents a 20-second pause.

IV PHYSICALIZING AN EMOTION

PLEASED. Physicalize pleased with your toes and heels. Have an immediate response. Go to the knees and move them around in the emotion. Add the pelvis. Complete the physicalization throughout the lower half of your body. Add the chest. Shoulders and elbows. If you need to heighten the physicalization in order to feel the emotion, do so. Fingers, knuckles, wrists. Every part of your body, from the neck down, is physicalizing pleased. Add the face. Physicalize pleased with your face. Heighten the entire physicalization. Check out your body parts to make sure they are all physicalizing pleased. Check in with yourself quickly and observe if you are feeling pleased. Stay out of your head. Now, observe your breathing. [20 sec.] Lose pleased. Shake it out as you walk. Take five long breaths, in through the nose and out through the mouth. [20 sec.] Speak gibberish out loud. [20 sec.] Walk around silently. [20 sec.] **CONFUSED.** Physicalize confused with your toes and heels. Add the knees. Pelvis. Chest. Shoulders and elbows. Hands. Face. Heighten the entire physicalization. Check out your body parts to make sure all of them are physicalizing confused. Check in with yourself quickly. Observe if you are feeling confused. Stay out of your head and just quickly observe. [20 sec.]. **Reality Check:** are you really doing confused feet or just assuming you are? Look at your feet and let them physically respond to these questions: Are you sure you want to take the next step? Which foot goes next? Which foot did you use last? Do you remember? Does it make a difference? Your feet are now physicalizing confused. There is a difference between really physicalizing and telling yourself you are physicalizing when you are not. Now, observe your breathing. Keep walking while physicalizing confused. [20 sec.] Lose confused. Shake it out as you walk. Take five long breaths, in through the nose and out through the mouth. [20 sec.] Speak gibberish out loud. [20 sec.]

Walk around silently. [20 sec.] **EMBARRASSED.** Embarrassed is not the same as feeling ashamed or guilty. Physicalize embarrassed with the whole lower half of your body, from the waist to your toes. Physicalize embarrassed from the waist to the neck as well. You're now physicalizing embarrassed from your neck to your toes. Add your face. Physicalize an embarrassed face. You're now physicalizing embarrassed with your whole body. Check in with yourself quickly. Observe if you are feeling embarrassed. Stay out of your head and just quickly observe. Now, observe your breathing. [20 sec.] Lose embarrassed. Shake it out as you walk. Take five long breaths, in through the nose and out through the mouth. [20 sec.] Speak gibberish out loud. [20 sec.] Walk around silently. [20 sec.] **DISGUSTED.** Physicalize disgusted with the whole lower half of your body. Add the upper half of your body, including your face. You're now physicalizing disgusted with your whole body. Check in with yourself quickly. Observe if you are feeling disgusted. Stay out of your head and just quickly observe. Now, observe your breathing. [20 sec.] Lose disgusted. Shake it out as you walk. Take five long breaths, in through the nose and out through the mouth. [20 sec.] Speak gibberish out loud. Walk around silently. [20 sec.] **TRIUMPHANT.** Physicalize triumphant with the whole lower half of your body. Add the upper half of your body, including your face. You're now physicalizing triumphant with your whole body. Check in with yourself quickly. Observe if you are feeling triumphant. Stay out of your head and just quickly observe. Now, observe your breathing. [20 sec.] Lose triumphant. Shake it out as you walk. Take five long breaths, in through the nose and out through the mouth. [20 sec.] Speak gibberish out loud. [20 sec.] Walk around silently. [20 sec.] **FURIOUS.** Immediately physicalize furious with the whole body. Check in with yourself quickly. Observe if you are feeling furious. Stay out of your head and just quickly observe. Now, observe your breathing. [20 sec.] Lose furious. Shake it out as you walk. Take five long breaths, in through the nose and out through the mouth. [20 sec.] Speak gibberish out loud. [20 sec.] Walk around silently. [20 sec.] **TERRIFIED.** Immediately physicalize terrified with the whole body. Check in with yourself quickly. Observe if you are feeling terrified. Stay out of your head and just quickly observe. Now, observe your breathing. [20 sec.] Lose terrified. Shake it out as you walk. Take five long breaths, in through the nose and out through the mouth. [20 sec.] Speak gibberish out loud. [20 sec.] Walk around silently. [20 sec.] **EROTIC.** Immediately physicalize erotic with the whole body. Check in with yourself quickly. Observe if you are feeling erotic. Stay out of your head and just quickly observe. Now, observe your breathing.

Before taking a break, lose the emotion by doing a **Step-Out**.

You are now physicalizing the emotions instantaneously. If you don't notice that your breathing is different with different emotions, you are probably not physicalizing completely. This will not be true for minimal emotion changes within the same emotion family. For example, your breathing will not be very different when physicalizing happy compared to amused. Some of the above choices are really attitudes and are included because attitudes of short duration, such as the length of a beat, may be physicalized in the same way as emotions. Practicing instantaneous emotion physicalizations is recommended.

Step #5: Make five choices:

▶ Select an activity with objects/props that has a beginning, middle, and end—for example, get dressed or clean a room. You will use real or invisible (space) props.

▶ Add a circumstance to the activity that would introduce an emotion and allow you to have strong feelings about doing this activity—for example, dressing in a locker room for a championship game or preparing a house for a wedding reception. Do not choose a circumstance that requires urgency.

▶ Select a turning point that would require you to undo the activity. For example, the wedding has been called off, so the house can return to normal; the game has been canceled, so the athlete can change back to street clothes.

▶ Choose how you will hear about the turning point. For example, you receive a telephone call or text; someone (imaginary) enters and briefly communicates the necessary information; whoever is reading the directions provides it.

▶ Select two emotions: one emotion for what your character is feeling during the activity before the turning point and a second emotion for what your character is feeling during the undoing of the activity after the turning point.

You are now ready to do the exercise. Before "Action," walk around and physicalize your first emotion (prior to turning point) with your whole body. You have one minute to physicalize. Feet. Knees. Pelvis. Chest. Shoulders. Arms. Hands. Face. Whole body. Places. Action. [Allow about 10-20 seconds between sentences.] Keep physicalizing with the whole body. Do the activity truthfully and communicate the emotion by how you handle the props. Assume there is an audience and you want to communicate the emotion by how you handle the objects. It's as if all the audience can see are your arms, your hands, and the objects. You want them to know how you feel. Feel what you are feeling and explore handling your props with that feeling. Every contact with a prop is an opportunity to show how you feel through that contact. Stay alert and take responsibility for every gesture. Every thing is done truthfully with a purpose. Every finger is an expression of that emotion: how you hold the prop, how you carry it, how you maneuver it, how you pull it, how you push it, how you adjust it, how you use it. Every moment, be very aware of how your hands and arms are showing your emotion through their handling of the objects [Allow 5 minutes]. As you complete the activity, activate the turning point—for example, answer or check your phone or see and hear the imaginary messenger delivering the information. Receive the communication and begin physicalizing your second emotion. There is no urgency. Take the time you need to feel the impact of the turning point and physicalize your second emotion. Allow your body to feel the emotion you chose. Physicalize that feeling throughout the whole body. You chose it before the scene; now choose it further by physicalizing it. While your whole body is physicalizing it, communicate it by how you handle the props, as you undo the original activity. Explore your use of the props with this feeling. Avoid relying on your face. Assume the audience can only see you from the elbows down. Anyone can show an emotion with the face; the actor uses his whole body. Stay alert and take responsibility for every gesture. Pay attention to what you are doing and check it out for yourself. Is what you are doing showing the audience the feeling? End it when you have undone the activity.

Let's lose the emotion by doing a **Step-Out**.

What impact did your emotional handling of the props have on your feeling of the emotions? It heightened it. Notice how easily you switched from the first emotion to the second.

You are now playing emotions by using the two components of physicalization: (1) using the whole body, and (2) using all props, all objects, and all business to show the emotion.

You can practice physicalizing an emotion at any time. Select an emotion and physicalize it with your whole body. Or, when an emotion spontaneously emerges, notice it, and complete it or top it off by physicalizing the whole body in response. You will notice the intensity of the emotion deepen. With practice your body develops a memory for just the right amount of physicalization. When you do an activity in your real life, physicalize an emotion and practice handling the objects with that emotion, or practice by improvising any activity with space props. Space props are recommended for their limitless application instead of relying on what real objects happen to be handy. With space props, whatever you need is right there. They are adaptable to inspiration and invention in the moment. They also offer an opportunity for you to pay more attention to the details of your object handling. Practice is important for reinforcing certain pathways in the brain while de-emphasizing others. Taking advantage of neuroplasticity, the necessary muscle commands for physicalizing an emotion become hard-wired into brain cells. Your brain becomes more efficient and focused on physicalizing. In other words, it turns the road less traveled into the beaten path. As Hamlet says to Gertrude, "For use almost can change the stamp of nature." With physicalization practice, your body eventually expresses the emotion on its own.

Voice

As long as you fully physicalize with your whole body, with or without business, any dialogue you have will be infused with the chosen emotion. If it isn't, you are not physicalizing with your whole body. The voice is a part of your body. Commit to the physicalization and the voice follows. See for yourself by physicalizing any emotion and saying lines (a monologue, the pledge of allegiance, song lyrics, improvised lines, etc.). While you say the lines, focus on your physicalization.

Green Screen

Physicalizing an emotion comes in very handy when you are acting in an empty space in front of a green screen with no one to play off of. Any scene partners who are not there because they are animated (or are avatars) will be added in post-production. Natalie Portman says that "green screen acting is the purest form of acting because you are inventing what's both outside of you and what's inside of you as an actor." When you don't have the contextual reality or mise-en-scène of what is really happening, feeling what you want your character to feel in that surreal world is no problem for the actor versed in physicalizing emotions. While there may not be anything to react to, just start the physicalization whenever you want the feeling to commence.

Feeling It?

Whether you feel the emotion or not is not the issue. It's a red herring. Feeling an emotion in an acting context is not the same as feeling an emotion in a life context. Real emotions occur without artificiality of circumstances. If you were really furious or really bawling in despair, you wouldn't be able to hit your marks, clip cues, play the subtext, climb your arcs, keep yourself from falling into the orchestra pit, or any of the other requirements of acting when you are feeling and playing emotions.

In performance, the emotions accompanying the desire for approval—and the fear of disapproval—from yourself, peers, audiences, directors, coaches, and teachers—are very real, but they are the actor's emotions, not the character's. They contribute more artificiality to the character's emotions, and the separation created by the artificiality doesn't allow you to really be in the character's emotions. Instead, you experience a secondary version of the emotion. After all, in the heat of any performance, you always know that you are acting, so how real can the emotions be? M. Louis Jouvet, one of the most influential figures of the French theater in the tweneith century, said, "On the stage an actor should hide what he feels and show what he doesn't." Kathleen Turner, who has played leading women opposite William Hurt, Jack Nicholson, and Michael Douglas, has strong feelings about this issue. "Real is not acting. Real pain, real sexuality, real getting hot turns people off. It gets in the way. People don't want to know that they are spying on someone." Mike Nichols said, "The idea that acting is *feeling*... is such nonsense and so useless and leads us into a corner of unintelligible people muttering."

The physicalization approach allows you to feel an emotion authentically within an acting context and provides you with the dexterity to do things with the emotion. The camera and the audience see you feeling the emotion, whether it's the lips turning upwards in a smile, the eyes narrowing in tension, or the furious cramming of clothes into your suitcase. Even if you could feel an emotion while performing exactly as you would feel it in real life, in the theater you would still need an instrument with which to express it for an audience. For camera acting, you can use any technique for feeling an emotion. If the technique is successful, the camera will catch it, but will you have control over it to the point of being able to feel it at a particular intensity when you need to, or to climb an emotion arc, or to switch to another emotion on cue? In addition, if the shot is larger than a two shot, the camera may not catch it. Physicalization will lead you to feelings that are communicated and available for further artful use.

In other words, physicalization provides the necessary emotion in the moment and enables you to make that moment blossom. Once you are accomplished with physicalization, it requires no preparation time. The importance of this cannot be overestimated. James Gandolfini, talking about playing Tony Soprano says, "When you're doing TV it's one scene right after another one. So, you have to learn to prepare very quickly because in one scene you'll be talking to your son and in the next scene you'll be beating somebody up, in the next scene you'll be making love to your wife, and so it's this constant change of emotions all through the day and you have to be able to shift very quickly."

When you physicalize the emotion, make sure you're using the whole body. If you only physicalize with different parts of the body (only arms and hands gesticulating angrily or only a frightened face), you will be *indicating*. Not good. In his book *Bambi vs. Godzilla*, David Mamet gives examples of indicating: "John Barrymore flinches to indicate surprise; Bela Lagosi narrows his eyes to indicate malevolence; Danny Kaye smiles to indicate charming harmlessness." In the past, actors indicating emotions helped to discredit the idea of playing a preselected emotion. This has limited generations of actors. Directors' notes to play this or that emotion came to be known as the dreaded "result" direction. Instead of dreading this note, the actor should understand that the director is asking for another choice and be able to offer it.

Physicalizing an emotion is best understood by doing the training steps and then bringing it to an actual scene where you want the character to feel and communicate a specific emotion. "As in combat, as in sex," David Mamet has said, "the theoretical is all well and good if one's a commentator, but the thing itself can actually be understood only through experience." A more thorough training in physicalizing emotions can be found in my *Book On Acting: Improvisation Technique for the Professional Actor in Film, Theater & Television*.

Optional

A simple and optional exercise will assist you in becoming more adept at recognizing the physicalization of specific emotions and expand your awareness of multiple emotions. It will also help you when selecting emotion choices. When you begin your day, ask yourself, "How are you?" Select the most perfect word to describe your mood. As you name it, observe your physicalization. Notice how your body parts feel, especially your limbs, stomach, chest, and face. Also notice your posture, your walk, how you handle objects. After a few days, do this exercise at bedtime also. After a few more days, ask and answer the question anytime you are aware of feeling anything. Just feel it, name it, and observe your body's physicalization. Be a witness, not a judge or a victim. "Just the facts, Ma'am, just the facts." Doing this exercise will pay off as you acclimate yourself to your new tool: physicalizing an emotion. This exercise includes a bonus for when you are feeling negative emotions, as it can be a fruitful beginning to learning to cope with them and also improve how you feel.

You will find Physicalizing an Emotion suggested as a tool in some of the solutions in the entries **Play the Story**, p. 97; **Make the Exposition Compelling**, p. 116; **Make a Monologue Compelling**, p. 110; **Play a Specific Emotion**, p. 131; **Intensify an Emotion Instead of Flatlining**, p. 147; **Make a Sharp Transition from One Emotion to Another**, p. 141; **Cry**, p. 152; **Commit to the Moment**, p. 244; **Nail a Close-up (Speaking)**, p. 251; **Do a Contradictory or Contrasting Direction**, p. 126.

V

EMOTION ARC

An **Emotion Arc**—increasing the intensity of an emotion over the length of a speech, beat, monologue, or scene—is almost always compelling. An emotion arc requires no rehearsal time and is similar to playing a musical scale while considering how loud, how soft, how soon, how late. For example, the emotion might rise gradually to a frenzied crescendo. Playing an emotion arc requires the ability to physicalize an emotion [see Physicalizing an Emotion, p. 31].

Learning How to Do an Emotion Arc

To start, it helps to know the emotion notes on the scale. When choosing to do an emotion arc, find out where the scale begins and ends and what notes are available to you. To find the beginning of the scale, choose what you think would be the least intense version of the desired emotion. For example, if fear is the emotion you or the director wants you to arc, what is the least intense version of fear? Where does the emotion start? You might choose from: concerned, cautious, curious, nervous, or scared. Whatever you choose, review it to see if it can be lowered further (even less intense) without leaving the original emotional family. Among the five choices provided here, I would say that "curious" is the least intense, and I would complete the intensity order as follows: curious, concerned, cautious, nervous, and scared. In reviewing my choice of curious as the least intense, I would ask myself

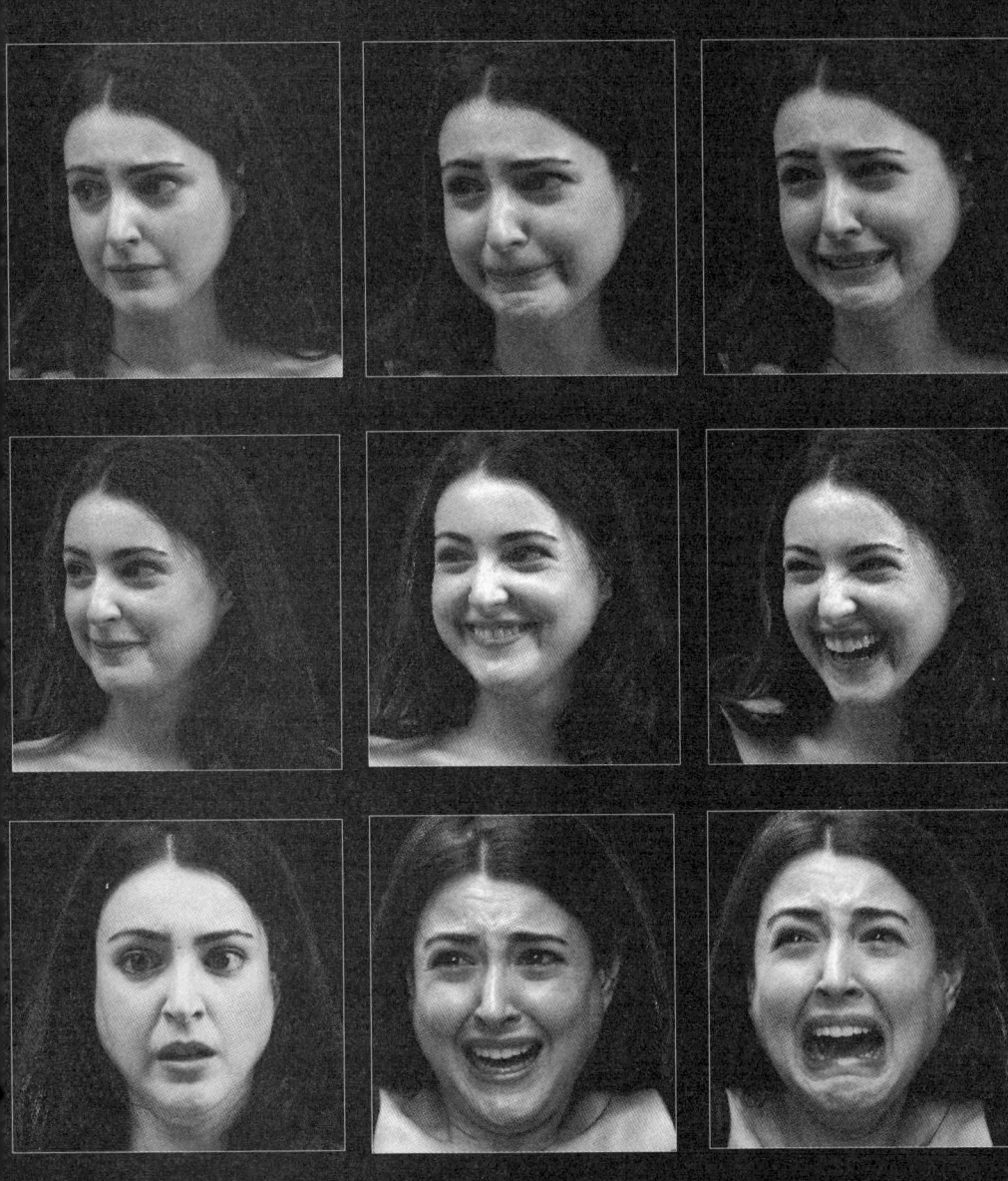

Selected stages of **Emotion Arcs** (sad, happy, and fear) demonstrated by Jacey Margolis.

if I could go lower than curious. How do I know there is something to be curious about? I'm aware of it. Aware becomes my new lowest-level feeling for the fear arc: aware, curious, concerned, cautious, nervous, and scared. Next, choose the feeling of highest intensity for the fear arc. I might choose terrified or horrified. The fear arc (or musical scale), as we have constructed it so far, is now: aware, curious, concerned, cautious, nervous, scared, terrified, and horrified. There will always be other levels of feeling that can fit between the lowest and highest levels. In this example, you might add: apprehensive, alarmed, frightened, worried. It is not necessary to add these other levels, but you may do so. When selecting the least and most intense choices, double-check that you haven't inadvertently moved into another emotion family.

You have just constructed, on paper, a complete fear arc. Select the level or intensity that you feel is appropriate for your character at the beginning of the designated text. You will start your emotion arc there. The level from which you start will be determined by what's happening in the scene, the director's input, and your instincts in the moment. For example, in the script, your fear arc doesn't begin until you innocently open a closet to get your jacket and a body falls out. You wouldn't start that fear arc at aware, but at something way more intense—scared, frightened, or alarmed. Regardless of the level you choose to start your arc, physicalize it with your whole body [Physicalizing an Emotion, p. 31] and heighten the physicalization in gradations as the scene proceeds. (How to heighten the physicalization is covered in the next paragraph.) You will thereby create an arc of the original emotion. Although you do not have to know the names of the levels of feeling you will be passing through, and you do not have to go through every level, an awareness of them from writing your complete arc on paper will help to acclimate your mind to what kind of journey it will be. All you are doing is heightening the feeling in the body. It's best to raise the intensity one or two levels at a time. You do not have to pre-select the level at which you will complete the arc. The feeling at the end will be determined in the moment. It may or may not be near the top of the arc (highest intensity). If you or the director feel it needs to end at a higher or lower intensity level, you can make the adjustment for the next take, rehearsal, or performance. You may also decide to climb the arc faster and go higher, or climb slower and not go as high. These controls are available to you when you physicalize emotions.

To heighten the physicalization, whatever your body parts are doing, let them do more of it. For example, with the fear arc, you will notice that your body is tense. Let it be more tense, even to the point of being rigid at the top of your arc (terrified or horrified). Your mouth may be open; open it more. Your eyes may feel fully open; open them a little more and try pushing them out and forward. Your breathing might feel shallow, with emphasis on the inhales; try making each inhale more emphatic by starting it abruptly. If your body feels like it's being pulled backwards, take a step backwards every time you do an emphatic inhale. You have to take charge of finding out how you can heighten the physicalization. If you practice doing emotion arcs, they will come easily and spontaneously, without you having to think of the individual body parts and what they do. Practice is also helpful for controlling the speed with which you go up your arc. You don't want to go too high too quickly, because it robs a scene of momentum and leaves you with the challenge of sustaining a very high intensity for longer than is necessary. Reaching the top of your arc halfway through the beat or scene makes the subsequent events in the scene seem less important because they have no further emotional impact on the character. Your rate of ascent should be influenced by the length of the speech, beat, or scene. You may never have the opportunity to play a complete emotion arc in performance, however, like a musical scale, learning and practicing them improves your facility and prepares you for when you need to climb an emotion arc of any length.

You can spontaneously choose the cues for heightening from one level to the next in the moment. The cues may be something you see or hear in the scene or your reactions to what you are saying or what you mean. Also, stay alert for any spontaneous heightening of the feeling on your part and use that as a solid cue to sustain the new level until you heighten it again. In other words, go with it! Stay alert and take advantage of anything going on in the scene to motivate and initiate your heightening. When you reach a new level, use it as a springboard to go higher. The length of the scene or beat determines the duration of your arc. Just keep heightening the physicalization as you go. There are times when it's suitable to not always be heightening; you can plateau (flatline) at any level of intensity for as long as feels right—until you feel a cue, in the moment, to go up to the next intensity level. While it is all right to plateau from time to time, you should never go backwards on the arc by lessening the intensity to a previously reached level. Stay on your current intensity level (plateauing) until you go higher. Whatever level you are on at any moment is your new starting place; everything from then on should be higher. Whether you are going *up, up, up* or *up, plateau (sustain), up* will be determined by you in the moment, based on what you are feeling, your lines, and what's going on in the scene.

Heightening your physicalization and creating your arc can be enhanced by your use of objects. For example, you can go from searching through your backpack with cautious hands to searching with desperate hands. The rest of your body is also physicalizing the change from cautious to desperate. If the physicalization is provided by only the hands, that's indicating. Physicalize with the whole body and climb your arc. Don't tell us what you are feeling. Show us.

As long as you fully physicalize with your whole body, with or without business, any dialogue you have will be infused with the emotion at that intensity level. Commit to the physicalization and the voice follows.

> You will find Emotion Arc suggested as a tool in some of the solutions in the entries **Make the Exposition Compelling**, p. 116; **Make a Monologue Compelling**, p. 110; **Intensify an Emotion Instead of Flatlining**, p. 147; **Cry**, p. 152; **Nail a Close-Up (Speaking)**, p. 251; **Improve Your Self-Tapes**, p. 259.

VI

UMBRELLA ARC

A character whose emotions don't develop or change in a scene is static and not terribly interesting. Frequently, a skillful writer or actor will create an **Umbrella Arc**. An umbrella arc takes your character on a particular emotional journey depicting a significant behavioral, psychological, or emotional change. Umbrella arcs occur over a limited duration (a speech, beat, or scene). There are two kinds of umbrella arcs. The first is based on a sense of movement or direction for the character. Examples include "coming back from defeat," "loss of illusion," and "celebrating power." Another kind of umbrella arc has the character revealing a set of related but different feelings, in other words, one state of mind that has multiple emotional components, like a psychological concept. For example, a character might react to one set of circumstances by experiencing and feeling one of the following umbrella arcs: "betrayal," "denial," "inundation," "self-pity,"or "abandonment." Within each umbrella arc are different emotions, and, in conjunction with each other, they fulfill the premise of the umbrella's name. If a writer has written three consecutive beats to reveal that your character is experiencing abandonment, each beat might require your character to communicate feelings from a different emotion family, for example, (beat 1) angry, (beat 2) scared, (beat 3) lonely. The buildup of these three consecutive beats forms the umbrella arc. In conjunction with the given circumstances and the dialogue, the umbrella arc communicates that your character is experiencing abandonment. The word "abandonment" will not appear in the text. It's your interpretation of what the writer intends for the character.

What a character is going through in a speech, beat, or scene often cannot be reduced to just one emotion, attitude, or action. An umbrella arc is a blueprint for how to express the various facets of your character's experience over a specific period of time. Use the text and given circumstances to lead you to an interpretive choice. What is the writer revealing about the emotional, attitudinal, or behavioral state of the character in the part of the scene you are working on? What is the character feeling or going through? Does your choice just repeat information in the dialogue, or is it an interpretation of how the character is feeling or the character's behavior? Acting is not about what you say. It's about what you do with the words you say, what the character is going through emotionally, the behavior of the character. When neither the script nor your interpretation suggests an umbrella arc, you should not arbitrarily impose one just to make the scene more interesting. It won't work because it will not be a suitable part of the whole.

In any scene, writers attempt to present more than what is happening on the surface. How many points can they score with the scene? Allow me to make up a short monologue to demonstrate my point.

```
Husband and wife at dinner table.

HUSBAND: You won't believe what happened to
me today. I come out of lunch with the boss,
we get in the car and pull out of the lot,
and a dog jumps in front of the car. Splat!
There's a little girl standing there and she
starts screaming. We get out of the car and
the dog is alive but a real mess. There's
blood everywhere. A crowd forms and everyone
```

```
is screaming at me. The little girl is crying
hysterically. And I see my boss just watching
me to see what I was going to do.
```

Aside from the events recounted by the husband, what might the writer have intended to reveal about him in this monologue? Depending on the rest of the script and the husband's character arc for the whole script, we have many choices.

Here are three:

> ▶ The husband is under a great deal of pressure and is not handling it well. As the script proceeds, he is going crazy. We could interpret the monologue as the author's device to reveal that the husband is feeling **tormented** or **haunted**.

> ▶ The husband suspects his wife is cheating on him and it's his part of the whole script to be feeling increasingly **betrayed**. The writer is using the monologue to reveal that he is feeling betrayed by everyone and everything.

> ▶ The husband has been through a great deal of trouble. He is coming back, overcoming adversity, and will do something heroic later in the script. The writer is using the monologue to reveal that he is **coming back from defeat**.

All three of these interpretive choices are umbrella arcs. The husband's story beyond the monologue—both before and after—will determine your interpretive choice.

After determining your choice, write it at the top of a column. Underneath it, list all the feelings that you think a person has when experiencing that choice. There is no right or wrong. There are only the feelings you can think of that belong under that umbrella. The top choice is called an umbrella because all the feelings have to fit underneath it.

For instance:

Tormented/Haunted	Betrayed	Coming Back from Defeat
Possessed	Hurt	Defeated
Terrified	Angry	Victorious
Alarmed	Resentful	Happy
Nervous	Hateful	Defiant
Wary	Vindictive	Hopeful
Frightened	Suspicious	Courageous
Scared	Bitter	
Confused	Sad	
Distraught	Sarcastic	
Suspicious	Furious	

After making the list under your umbrella choice, rearrange the items in it according to level of intensity, from least to most intense. If your list includes emotions from different emotional families, arrange them from least to most intense within each family. The order of the families should be determined by your own sense of which comes first when one is feeling the top, or umbrella, choice. For instance:

Tormented/Haunted	Betrayed	Coming Back from Defeat
Confused	Hurt	Defeated
Wary	Sad	Hopeful
Suspicious	Suspicious	Courageous
Nervous	Resentful	Defiant
Distraught	Bitter	Victorious
Scared	Sarcastic	Happy
Frightened	Angry	
Alarmed	Vindictive	
Terrified	Furious	
Possessed	Hate	

VI UMBRELLA ARC

Look at the text and divide it into beats, labeling the beats from the choices on the list. Assign a different feeling choice to each beat. You do not have to use all the choices on the list, and you may add choices you hadn't previously thought of. You are choreographing the speech emotionally so that, if you performed the choices, the audience would see a character going through your umbrella arc choice.

Here are sample choices for the monologue. Try them out in order to experience how you are serving the umbrella choice. Read the lines out loud while you physicalize each beat choice. Note that the different umbrellas sometimes create different-sized beats.

Tormented / Haunted

Beat #1: Suspicious

You won't believe what happened to me today. I come out of lunch with the boss, we get in the car and pull out of the lot, and a dog jumps in front of the car.

Beat #2: Nervous

Splat! There's a little girl standing there and she starts screaming. We get out of the car and the dog is alive but a real mess. There's blood everywhere.

Beat #3: Scared

A crowd forms and everyone is screaming at me. The little girl is crying hysterically.

Beat #4: Possessed

And I see my boss just watching me to see what I was going to do.

In performance, you would be revealing a character who is tormented and haunted.

Betrayed

Beat #1: Bitter

You won't believe what happened to me today. I come out of lunch with the boss, we get in the car and pull out of the lot, and a dog jumps in front of the car.

Beat #2: Sarcastic (mockery)

Splat! There's a little girl standing there and she starts screaming. We get out of the car and the dog is alive but a real mess. There's blood everywhere. A crowd forms and everyone is screaming at me. The little girl is crying hysterically.

Beat #3: Hate

And I see my boss just watching me to see what I was going to do.

In performance, you would be revealing a character who is feeling betrayed.

Coming Back from Defeat

Beat #1: Defeated

You won't believe what happened to me today. I come out of lunch with the boss, we get in the car and pull out of the lot, and a dog jumps in front of the car. Splat! There's a little girl standing there and she starts screaming.

Beat #2: Courageous

We get out of the car and the dog is alive but a real mess. There's blood everywhere. A crowd forms and everyone is screaming at me. The little girl is crying hysterically.

Beat #3: Victorious

```
And I see my boss just watching me to see
what I was going to do.
```

In performance, you would be revealing a character who is coming back from defeat.

The actor is now making the text about more than the words themselves. There is nothing in the text about feeling tormented/haunted, betrayed, or coming back from defeat. Always assume that the writer is choosing to reveal something about the character in addition to what the character says. No matter what your choice is, we are still going to get what the character is saying. Keep in mind that any stage directions are clues to the writer's intent, not demands. Where they are placed, regardless of what they say, there will frequently be a beat change.

After making your interpretive choices and designating the beats, perform the choices spontaneously while you say the text. To achieve the spontaneity, simply improvise your acting by focusing on Physicalizing the Emotion [p. 31] for each beat choice. An Emotion Switch [Make a Sharp Transition from One Emotion to Another, Solution #1, p. 141] will take you from one beat to the next. Most of the beats in an umbrella arc are plateaued. When you plateau, there is room for variation within that chosen feeling unconstrained by an order of increasing intensity. Staying on your improvisational acting focus, physicalizing the emotion will create line readings that are slightly different in every performance or take. Pay no attention to line readings, only the continued physicalization of the emotion. If you do that, however you say the lines will serve your purpose, and your body, mind, and voice will be free to make discoveries every time you run it. In other words, how you say your lines will be improvised in the moment but always with the same emotion, regardless of intensity levels. Occasionally, you may decide to arc the emotion within any one beat. If you are arcing, just increase the intensity of the emotion's physicalization throughout the designated beat [Emotion Arc, p. 51]. How you travel up an arc is improvised. How you switch from one emotion to another when changing beats is improvised.

If an interpretive choice based on the writer's intention eludes you, keep breaking down the text. Look for clues and ask yourself questions. For instance, the sample monologue is about a car accident. What question can you ask about the car accident? "Well, how do I (the character) feel about the accident?" The surrounding text may yield a clue. In the case of the betrayed husband, "How do I (the character) feel about the fact that I am having dinner with my wife now that I suspect she's having an affair?" Whatever the situation, you can always ask yourself how your character feels about it.

The beat labels within any umbrella arc should be emotions or attitudes. If you are stymied when looking for the right one-word emotion or attitude, select a verb as a last resort and ask yourself: "How does my character feel about [verb]?" (for example: "How does my character feel about escaping?"). That should make it easier to arrive at an emotion choice. If a choice still eludes you, play that beat as if you are playing the verb or physicalize the verb as you would physicalize an emotion.

When considering what choice to make, use your body as well as your mind. Read the beat out loud with your prospective choice. Make sure that you physicalize the choice as well as trying out line readings with that choice.

Sample umbrella arcs and their breakdowns are found in Appendix A. They are useful guides in determining umbrella arcs for any dialogue or monologues beats. My students and clients find them to be valuable checklists for preparing script choices. When they are learning this approach to umbrella arcs, I encourage them to resist going

VI UMBRELLA ARC

directly to this appendix, which can keep them from developing their own muscles and creating new and unique arcs.

You will find Umbrella Arc suggested as a tool in some of the solutions in the entries **Make a Monologue Compelling**, p. 110; **Make the Exposition Compelling**, p.116; **Cry**, p. 152.

[top]: First rehearsal for cast of Comedy Central pilot *Special Unit*. Back row, left to right: Bryan Cranston (Director), Michael Aronin, Christopher Titus, Stephen Book (Creative Consultant), David Figlioli. Front row: Christopher Thornton, Debbie Lee Carrington.

[bottom]: On the set of *Special Unit*, left to right: Christopher Thornton, Michael Aronin, Christopher Titus, Debbie Lee Carrington, David Figlioli.

VII

MONOLOGUES: BREAKDOWN AND REHEARSAL

Scripts have a built-in rhythm. A structural device employed by the writer to hook the audience, the rhythm carries the audience through the script, building to the climax and conclusion. When a character has a monologue, the rhythm can potentially grind to a halt. Why would a writer choose to impede his own carefully constructed rhythm? He may deem it a valuable tradeoff to sacrifice movement for the opportunity to reveal something about the character, or he may believe that if the monologue is done the way he conceived it, the rhythm will not be impeded. Not only do many actors (and directors) fail to sustain the rhythm through the monologue, but they also cut their own throats with monologues, especially at auditions, because their understanding of what to do with the monologue is incomplete. The writer intends—and you should perform—every monologue to reveal something about the character that is not mentioned in the monologue. It could be as simple as revealing the character is angry or as complex as revealing the character is losing his illusions about his life.

Making the Choices

In order to understand what the writer intended, consider two possibilities. The first possibility is character revelation. The monologue shows us, or reveals, the character's emotional state or where he is on his character arc. For example, the character is feeling betrayed, victorious, abandoned, rebellious, or has come back from defeat. The second possibility is a story point response. Something significant occurs just before, during, or just after the monologue, and the purpose of the monologue is to show the audience the character's behavioral, emotional, or attitudinal response to that story point. The various responses of multiple characters to the same story point reveal their similarities and differences.

Determine whether the monologue fits the first or second possibility. This is easy. All you have to do is determine whether a story point occurs around the time of the monologue and your character knows about it. It may have occurred just prior to the monologue, within a few pages; just after the monologue, within a few pages; or at the same time as the monologue, probably in another location. If no story point occurs near or at the same time as the monologue, then the purpose of the monologue is character revelation.

Story points are crucial events that move the plot along: a crime, a discovery, a confession, a death, an opportunity, a decision. Without them, there would be no reason for all the text that follows. Scripts are generally constructed to move from one story point to the next. If a wife discovers her husband in bed with another woman, that's a story point. There may be pages of text until she decides to get a divorce (story point), more pages until she actually moves out (story point), more pages until she meets a new man (story point), and so on. Story points never occur in the past, only the present or, if the character knows it's about to happen, the immediate future. Suppose a scene is about Charlie finding out for the first time, that his mother committed suicide when he was a child. The moment he hears this information is a story point, but not her suicide itself. The story point would be named this way: Charlie discovers his mom killed herself. If you can't name the story point in a factual statement, it is not a story point.

When you can designate and name a story point near or in your monologue, you are ready to make an acting choice for the monologue. Ask yourself: "How does my character feel about [the story point]?" In the above example, how does Charlie's discovery that his mother killed herself make him feel? If the story point is a wife discovering her husband in bed with another woman, the three characters concerned will have different responses to it. For the wife, it might be shock, which changes to hurt and anger; for the husband, it might be embarrassment that changes to guilt; for the other woman, it might be happiness. Maybe she is his co-worker and wants to marry him, and she thinks the wife's arrival at this moment may break up the marriage. The actor chooses the response based on the actor's interpretation of the writer's intention.

If your monologue occurs near the story point, choose how your character feels about or responds to the story point and show that to the audience or camera while you say the lines of the monologue. Obviously, what you say in the monologue will influence your choice, but the monologue is about more than the words. The monologue is about your emotional response to the story point. Add to what you say by showing how you feel.

If there is no story point near the monologue, you are in the realm of character revelation. Choosing emotions for this kind of monologue is more difficult because, without a specific story point to respond to, there is more room for interpretation. The clues for making a good choice are in the monologue (sentence meanings, word choices or syntax, punctuation, stage directions) and in the given circumstances. What is the character feeling? Is your choice based on repeating what the character says or on your interpretation of one or more of these other clues in the monologue? Acting is not about what you say. It's about how you say it, which shows the audience what the character is going through emotionally. Monologues are always about feelings, not information. Use the text and the given circumstances to lead you to an interpretive choice of what the character is feeling, and then, in character, perform that choice spontaneously while you say the text.

Performing the Choices Spontaneously

You might make multiple emotion choices over the course of a monologue. If there is only one choice (for example, angry), the fastest and easiest way to make the monologue compelling is to intensify the emotion—in other words, arc it [see Emotion Arc, p. 51]. For anger, you might start the monologue playing irritated (low intensity) and become angrier as you proceed until, at the end, you are furious (high intensity). You can start the emotion arc at any intensity and leave it at any higher intensity (for example, annoyed to aggravated). An emotion arc will make a one-choice monologue more compelling. Find the one emotion the writer intended, arc it, and you will knock it out of the park. One-emotion monologues are usually not very long.

Some monologues may comprise several beats that each require a different emotion. Break the monologue into separate beats, each with its own emotion. Let the text of the beat (sentence meanings, word choices or syntax, punctuation, stage directions) and the given circumstances provide you with clues for your choice. With this approach, the length of text dedicated to playing one emotion choice determines a beat. If you are doing the whole monologue with one emotion choice, then the whole monologue is one beat. If you are doing two emotion choices, each choice is one beat, with a transition between the beats. Three beats have three emotion choices with two transitions, etc. The number of beats in the monologue is your interpretive decision. If you decide the monologue has multiple beats, make a sharp transition from one emotion to another [Make a Sharp Transition from One Emotion to Another, p. 141]. Emotion switches will make any monologue more compelling. In addition, you might choose to arc your choice for any single beat. Multiple beats of different emotions are usually employed by the writer to reveal where a character is on his character's arc for the whole script.

Look at the character's arc [see Appendix B for Sample Character Arcs, p. 269]. What is happening for the character at the time of the monologue? Consider as an example the character who suspects his wife is cheating on him. At this point in his character arc, maybe he is feeling increasingly betrayed by everyone, including his wife—a feeling that the writer intends the monologue to show. Based on this interpretation, you decide that the choice would be "betrayed." It's also possible that earlier in the story the character has been through a great deal of trouble. At the time of the monologue, he is overcoming adversity, and, later in the script, he will do something heroic. In this case you could interpret the writer is using the monologue to reveal that he is coming back from defeat. In these examples your character revelation choices for the whole monologue would be either "betrayed" or "coming back from defeat." Always assume that the writer is choosing to reveal something about the character in addition to what the character says. No matter what your choice is, whether the monologue is a story point response or a character revelation, we are still going to get what the character is saying.

If your choice is labeled with a word or phrase other than a single pure emotion or with multiple beats of different emotions, consider that you have chosen an umbrella arc. How to construct, rehearse, and perform umbrella arcs is covered in Umbrella Arcs [p. 57], Make the Exposition Compelling [p. 116], and Cry [p. 152].

Once you have picked your character revelation choice or story point response, get more specific with what you are going to do with that choice. For instance, do you just play that one emotional choice, for example, happy, on a plateau for the whole beat? Or do you arc it, starting with, let's say, pleased or amused and intensifying up to joyous? Does the monologue seem to comprise specific beats of different emotions, calling your attention to the possibility of a self-designed (umbrella) arc? Perhaps the monologue has beats of the same emotion, but each beat is at a different and specific intensity (for example, three beats of fear: cautious, frightened, terrified). How do you know which of these approaches will serve you best?

▶ If the monologue reads like one feeling all the way, with no significant beat changes, it could be a one-beat plateau of one emotion.

▶ Consider the rhythm of the sentences. Does the monologue have a natural rhythm that repeats itself while getting stronger, similar to the musical feeling you get from Ravel's *Bolero* or Jefferson Airplane's "White Rabbit"? That might suggest a one-beat arc of one emotion, simply increasing the intensity of that emotion throughout the monologue.

▶ Do you sense that there are shifts in emphatic feelings? The shifts will suggest multiple beats with emotion labels. Define your beats and select your emotions to match the feelings for each beat. Performing the monologue will require emotion switches.

▶ If you are considering multiple beats with emotion labels, stay alert to the possibility that you are dealing with an umbrella arc. Look at the whole monologue in relation to the given circumstances to see if the character is going through a behavioral or emotional change that reveals a sense of movement or direction (examples include coming back from defeat, loss of illusion, celebrating power). Is the character revealing a conceptual or complex feeling comprising multiple emotions (examples include betrayal, denial, abandonment, inundation)?

You see how many choices are available to you for any monologue. The actor is now making the monologue about more than the words, as the writer intended. There may be no mention in the monologue of feeling betrayed or coming back from defeat or whatever your choice is. This kind of interpretive analysis or script breakdown may be more in-depth than you bargained for. However, it's something to begin thinking about and exploring. Nothing is learned that isn't experienced, including these words.

How to Rehearse

You must be off book and know your lines cold. If you have determined the whole monologue to be one beat of one emotion, plateau, or arc, practice physicalizing the chosen emotion or physicalizing the emotion arc while saying the lines in the moment. Run it as many times as necessary until you are thoroughly physicalizing the choice and the lines flow easily. Make no attempt to retain line readings from one run-through to the next.

If you have determined the whole monologue to have more than one beat you do not have to remember all the beat choices, because you are only going to be rehearsing one beat at a time. You can check your script where you have written the beat choices to tell you what choice is next. Physicalize the first beat choice, using Physicalizing an Emotion [p. 31] or Emotion Arc [p. 51]. Rehearse the first beat only, and repeat it as many times as necessary until you are thoroughly physicalizing the choice and the lines flow easily. Make no attempt to retain line readings from one run-through to the next. Treat each run-through of the beat as an improv where the lines are scripted and not to be changed while the acting is improvised. The improvisational acting focus of each run-through is physicalizing an emotion or emotion arc. Each run-through will come out a little different. Your goal is to always play that emotion choice while being open to spontaneous differences in intensity, timing, or inflection.

When the first beat is done, approach the second beat the same way. When you're done with the second beat and its emotion choice, do a run-through of the first two beats, and spontaneously make the transition between the two beats. Do it in rhythm, in other words, don't hesitate or stop to make decisions or to create gradual transitions [Make a Sharp Transition from one Emotion to Another, Solution #1—Emotion Switch, p. 141]. Do as many run-throughs as necessary until you are successfully maintaining each beat with its choice and easily handling the transition. Then, one at a time, rehearse the remaining beats in the same thorough fashion, always ending with a run-through of the previous beats and the beat you have been working on. Continue this process for every beat until the end of the monologue. The first run-through to include the last beat can be the final run-through. Further run-throughs can be for practice, if needed. For an experiment, after you have thoroughly rehearsed with this approach, you might do an additional run-through or a take where you deliberately choose to forget about your choices and just play the monologue in the moment and go with it. Think of it this way: plan (the breakdown), perfect (rehearsal process), forget (just go with it). This experimental/go with it run-through or take is sometimes the best one, and it usually ends up almost identical to the breakdown choices. Being free of the obligation to do what you want to do (the breakdown choices), you end up doing exactly what you want to do.

Even though you did not have to remember all the beat choices when you started this process, your body has now learned them be-

VII MONOLOGUES: BREAKDOWN AND REHEARSAL

cause of the work on each beat and each run-through. In this process, the body will always remember the choices.

If you are working on a monologue that requires crying, see the entry **Cry**, p. 152, with special instructions for Rehearsing the Final Sub-beat, p. 163.

You will find Monologues: Breakdown and Rehearsal suggested as a tool in some of the solutions in the entries **Make a Monologue Compelling**, p. 110; **Make the Exposition Compelling**, p. 116; **Cry**, p. 152.

George Carlin receiving his star on the Hollywood Walk of Fame with his acting coach Stephen Book.

ALL THE STUFF

*I have learned to relish the challenge
in translating a director's demand for quick results
into a working process that helps me deliver them.*
—Laura Linney

*The more technique you have,
the less you have to worry about it.
The more technique there is,
the less there is.*
—Pablo Picasso

[top]: Directors of the Spolin Theater Game Center: Robert Martin (Technical), Viola Spolin (Artistic), and Stephen Book (Executive).

[bottom]: Stephen Book and Lillian Gish discussing D. W. Griffith's use of improvisation in the silent film era.

VIII

DOING

From Stanislavsky onward, all of the widely used contemporary techniques of acting emphasize that "acting is doing." Stanislavsky referred to doing in two different ways, at times focusing on physical actions and activities—for example, cleaning, cooking, dressing, building, or repairing. At other times emphasizing how a character solves the problems posed in the play—for example, warning, seducing, teasing, or punishing. Viola Spolin extended the range of doing to include improvisation that may or may not be related to a character's desired outcome or a character's objective or intention. Examples of Spolin's improvisations include stage whispering, gibberish, or other vocal concentrations; conflict; agreement; and physicalization. Spolin also placed a special emphasis on the original form of doing, physical activities. As I developed Improvisation Technique for scripted acting, I added a second phrase to that widely used maxim: "Acting is doing...and there is always more to do." The entries in this section offer solutions to specific needs or directors' requests that require more doing.

[Reminder: Many of the solutions throughout the book involve the **Secret Magic Stuff** that I find to be most effective with the quickest results. Those solutions are highlighted by a star ★.]

WHEN YOU NEED TO

PLAY DRUNK

★ Solution #1 — Moving Halo

This solution also provides controls for maintaining, increasing, or diminishing intensity as the scene progresses.

Step #1: Stand still and imagine a golf ball about 4 to 6 inches above your head. The golf ball is made of titanium and is a super magnet or force field that attracts your body. Keeping your feet flat on the ground, let your body respond to the pull of the magnet. You should now be feeling taller.

Step #2: Imagine the ball moving in circles above your head, like a halo (with a diameter of about 4 or 5 inches). You can control the speed of the ball's movement. It should at first take about 6 to 10 seconds for the ball to complete the circle. Keep the circle going, allowing your body to respond to the magnet's pull. You should now be feeling your body listing (like on a ship) as it moves in a circular motion. If your performance requires walking while drunk, practice walking while imagining the ball moving above you. If you have dialogue, practice saying your lines at the same time. Stay focused on the moving ball and responding to it physically as you say the lines. Allow your body's movement to influence and affect the line readings; let the line readings be a spontaneous response to how your body feels while focused on the ball. Do not hold on to predetermined line readings, and don't stop responding to the moving ball. Just stay focused on the process, allowing your body to respond to the moving ball as you say your lines. They will come out sounding drunk at an intensity matching the extent of your body's listing.

Step #3: You can adjust for how drunk you want to play. An especially powerful adjustment, which I highly recommend, is to arbitrarily stop the ball's rotation and then immediately resume it, but in the opposite direction. As you make this change, keep allowing your body to respond to the magnetic pull. Change the direction of the ball's rotation as often as you like. The more you do it, the drunker you will be. If you feel dizzy while doing it, that's the same dizziness one feels when drunk. Use it! Here are some other adjustments for how drunk you want to play: Increase (for more drunk) or decrease (for less drunk) the diameter of the halo (for example, a diameter 1 inch for least drunk, 8 inches for shit-faced and hardly able to take a step). Increase (for more drunk) or decrease (for less drunk) the height of the moving ball (halo) above your head or the speed of the ball's rotation. These adjustments will help you to become more or less drunk over the course of a scene. If you feel you need a stronger sense of the magnetic pull, you can increase the size of the ball (for example, from a golf ball to a baseball). *When making these adjustments, it's important to remember that the ball is always moving and your body is always responding.* Stay focused on the moving ball. A suggested approach to getting drunker during a scene can have three phases: (1) a ball circles slowly above your head; (2) the ball moves a little faster; (3) the ball arbitrarily stops and reverses direction frequently.

Solution #2 — Spinning

Ask the director to cue you 10 seconds prior to "Action." When cued, you will stand on your mark and spin around in a circle like a whirling dervish for 10 seconds. Before the director calls "Action," you will stop and tell the director, "Ready." Struggle with your dizziness as you play the scene. This was the approach Dennis Hopper used with great effect as the town drunk in *Hoosiers*. For the theater, do the spinning off stage for 10 seconds prior to your drunken entrance. This solution can be very effective for drunken entrances, but you will have very little actor's control of your drunken dizziness, which will wear off as the scene proceeds.

WHEN YOU NEED TO

PLAY STONED

★ Solution

Sitting or standing, imagine a deflated balloon inside your head. Feel it inflating slowly with helium. Allow your whole body, including your face, to respond to what you are imagining and feeling—go with it! Practice responding to the inflating balloon while walking. If you have dialogue, practice saying your lines while responding. Don't be concerned with line readings. Just say your lines while staying focused on the balloon and the resulting feelings. Enjoy it!

Even though what you are imagining and the process of imagining are both in your head, don't cut off the rest of your body from the process. Allow your body to go with it. You can control the speed and intensity of getting high by controlling the rate of the balloon's inflation. You can pause the inflation at any point for as long as you want, and you can choose to get higher by resuming it. You can come down by gradually deflating the balloon.

If the balloon is fully inflated and you want to get higher, have another hit with an imaginary or space joint, and imagine three holes in the top of your head and three balls rolling around up there that you try to get into the holes without using your hands. Go with it. Don't let go of the balloon inside your head. When you want to come down, forget about the balls and come down gradually by deflating the balloon in increments. Allow your body to respond to the deflating until you are back to not being high.

WHEN YOU NEED TO

PICK UP THE PACE

"Be quick *but don't hurry*" was a phrase used during practice by the legendary and 10-time national champion UCLA basketball coach **John Wooden**. It has great application to acting. Ask the director if it's just you or everyone in the scene who has to pick up the pace.

Solution #1 — Italian Run-Through

If everyone has to pick up the pace, suggest an Italian Run-Through of the scene. In an Italian Run-Through, everyone has to do the scene as fast as humanly possible. It will be as if everyone is on the strongest dose of speed, speaking all their lines and doing all their business as fast as they can. The words should race out of everyone's mouth. Don't even let the other person finish a sentence. There's no time for acting choices or pauses of any kind. From out front it will look ridiculous, like a foreign movie speeded up. That's why the students at Juilliard always referred to it as an Italian Run-Through.

During the Italian Run-Through, you experience how fast the scene can actually be done without leaving out any lines or business. Your body will now bring that muscle memory of the scene's potential speed to doing it again with the acting included and no mandate to do it as fast as possible. The scene will have a quicker pace while not seeming speeded up because your body will skip over or remove what is not necessary. After an Italian Run-Through, there are usually no more unnecessary pauses, slow line readings, labored transitions, or slow cue pickups.

Solution #2 — Clip Cues

If it's you who has to pick up the pace, clip your cues. Start your lines on the last word of your cue, as the word's last letter is being pronounced, or immediately following the last word of your cue. There should be no space between the last word of the cue and the first word of your line.

Solution #3 — Specificity

If it's you who has to pick up the pace, sometimes it's not really that you are too slow, but that what you are doing is not detailed enough. Your acting is not deserving of the time you're giving it. What you are doing might be too generic. Review your choices and look for places to be more specific. Think about how you can fill or play with moments instead of giving them lip service. Provide variety wherever you can. Divide any lengthy beats into shorter beats with new choices and transitions. Look at your rhythms—can they be changed? Can you be better connected to your inner life or to a subtext? If you make these changes, you will end up doing more in the same amount of time, and it will seem to pass more quickly.

Solution #4 — Justification

Whether it's you or everyone who has to pick up the pace, add a justification for speaking and doing all your business faster. You can invent and add a given circumstance to the scene. For example, your character has just found out that she has been invited on a free trip to Paris because her friend's husband had to cancel at the last minute. The taxi is here to take you to the airport, and you must leave immediately to get to the airport in time. This new circumstance will allow you to play the scene at a quicker pace in an organic fashion. Perhaps you don't need to add the trip to Paris; it is enough that you have a taxi waiting to take you somewhere and the meter is running. If everyone has to pick up the pace, the new circumstance needs to affect everyone, or everyone needs their own individual new circumstance.

WHEN YOU NEED TO

DO A WALK-AND-TALK

A walk-and-talk is a shot where you have dialogue and, perhaps, business while walking and stopping and walking. This kind of shot is usually filmed with a Steadicam following you and the other character. Actors frequently feel inundated with all the logistics. You worry about doing any business and dialogue in the designated and blocked spots or while walking. Bradley Whitford recalls the anxiety provoked by walk-and-talks: "We got people who were so scared of doing walk-and-talks on *The West Wing* that we would intentionally fuck up the first take early. It's relaxing—it would tell them, "Oh, you can fuck up here.""

★ Solution

After receiving the blocking and dialogue timing directions, rehearse the shot by yourself. Break down the blocking into sections based on doing something in each section. Here is an example of an extremely complicated walk-and-talk: getting up from your office desk; crossing to another desk; picking up a file; crossing to the copy machine while looking at the file; operating the copy machine; crossing to the coffee table; picking up a muffin; returning to the copying machine; and picking up the copy. Rehearse each section, one at a time, without dialogue. Starting with the first section, getting up from your desk, say out loud, "Begin." Get up from your desk and say out loud, "End." Repeat this section: say, "Begin," get up from your desk, and say, "End." Move on to the second section, say, "Begin," cross to the other desk, and say, "End." Repeat. Move on to the third section, say, "Begin," pickup file, and say, "End." Repeat. Continue this process through the remaining sections, saying "Begin" and

"End" out loud and where they belong. When you have twice completed all the sections, run the whole sequence once without saying "Begin" and "End." You will discover that you have it and don't need to think about it. Your body will take care of all the blocking and business by itself and you only have to focus on matching your lines to the moves. Ask the other actor to rejoin you and run it with her with dialogue. Tell the director you are ready. Enjoy playing the scene. Not every actor can be in an Aaron Sorkin show. An earlier version of Begin and End was created by Viola Spolin to bring out more physical details in a scene and to pick up the pace.

WHEN YOU NEED TO

SEDUCE ANOTHER CHARACTER

To seduce, you have to be active, not passive.

★ Solution #1 — Physical Contact

Rehearse and/or perform the scene with a private rule only you know about: Every time you speak, you must find a way to have one part of your body make physical contact with one part of the other character's body. You should vary these contacts so various parts of your body are in contact with various parts of the other's body. Just touching someone's shoulder every time you speak is not going to do it. Making sure the operative word in your own thinking or focusing is *contact* and not *touch* will help you. Obviously, the contact should be appropriate. Do not grab the other's crotch or the like. Keep discovering (improvising) new ways of making contact. Mix it up, examples include, toes to toes, chin to shoulder, back to back, etc. Avoid limiting your contacts to the same body parts. The contact should last as long as you are speaking. Always allow the contacts to influence how you say your lines in the moment. If you can't make physical contact, you are not allowed to speak. If what you are saying goes on beyond a sentence or two, the equivalent of a short monologue, change your physical contact every time you express a new thought. When the other character speaks, you do not have to initiate physical contact.

If you follow this rule in a rehearsal, for the next run-through, performance, or take, drop the rule necessitating the contact every time you speak. Instead, allow your body to be selective and make contact when it wants to. The experience of having done it every time you spoke has impacted your muscle memory. Your body has learned something about the scene from the rehearsal. Now you have to get out of the body's way and let it show you how it wants to play the scene. Your body knows how; your brain does not. Your body may choose to retain some of the contacts from the way you rehearsed the scene, or there may be new contacts or no contacts at all. Let your body spontaneously determine what it wants to do at any moment in the scene. Don't censor. Don't plan ahead. Go with it.

Physical contact heightens the characters' involvement with each other. If the scene is about a seduction, the seduction will be heightened and highlighted. The challenge of how to make the physical contact creates a crisis to which your body will respond with focused energy in the moment. Rehearsing the scene while you focus on improvising physical contacts breaks previous patterns that may have become labored or passive. It also re-infuses spontaneity into the scene while setting up maximum potential for further discoveries about the seduction.

★ Solution #2 — Attitude Line

Adjust your character's attitude for the scene so that your desire for the other is heightened and emphasized. To do this, take on a specific attitude line for the scene. The attitude line is either "I love women" or "I love men," depending on who's seducing who. For how to take on the attitude line, see Attitude Line Process [p. 13].

Solution #3 — Manipulation

Take a more active role in rehearsals of the scene, as if you are a second director, and get the other character to unbutton her blouse or remove his shirt during the scene. You might discover in yourself certain behaviors, attitudes, or manipulations that you can retain in the performance.

Solution #4 — Real Seduction

In 1972, I witnessed Lee Strasberg suggest this approach to heighten a seduction scene in the Directors Unit at the Actors Studio. Lee called it an improvisation that he then defined as "behaving logically and believably in a situation that somewhat parallels the situation in the text." He felt the improv challenge must be real in order to arouse the actor's conviction.

If you decide to use Strasberg's approach, make a decision that you, not your character, are going to do whatever it takes to seduce the actor playing the other character. Using the components of the rehearsal or performance process, including the characters, the text, props, the set, clothes, the blocking, business, other cast members, the crew, backstage, craft services, dressing rooms, really seduce the other actor. The seduction may be called your task and it should only be done during a rehearsal of the scene, including rehearsal breaks or the setting up of a shot. You might find yourself discovering all kinds of opportunities for embracing the other actor or taking the seduction further. The other actor will then really have to deal with that, heightening the drama inherent in the scripted scene.

You can explore the intensity of your seduction by attaching a time limit to the task. For example, if you want sex, it must happen in your dressing room right now or on the next break (most intense), immediately after you're both excused from the set or rehearsal at the end of the workday (intense), or after the cast party next week (less intense). Don't try to improve your performance of the seduction by working on your task outside of that scene's rehearsal or shooting.

At the Actors Studio in 1972, no one questioned Strasberg's approach. Today, most actors would look at it differently. Adopt it at your own risk.

WHEN YOU NEED TO

THINK ON CAMERA OR STAGE

Bob Hoskins said, "When the lens is that close to your face, it can see you *think,* the camera can see you think." Michael Caine adds, "You must be thinking every moment because the camera looks into your mind, and the audience sees what the camera sees. The real key is in your mental transmission. If the mind is in overdrive, the body is headed in the right direction."

When you need to be seen thinking, a solid approach is to improvise the thinking by using Question and Answer Railroad Tracks [see p. 3]. The audience will not know what you are thinking, but they will know that you are thinking real thoughts. Using this tool is a great way to get into thinking *as* the character instead of *for* the character. You will discover how your character thinks and what your character's thoughts are in the moment. Regardless of the number of takes, rehearsals, or performances, the thinking will always be spontaneous as you improvise new thoughts each time.

When using any of these solutions, do your thinking authentically. Don't add any acting to it to make sure the camera sees it. When Tammy Grimes asked James Stewart, "What is the difference between film acting and stage acting?," he replied, "The difference is, on stage, you use your whole body to express something. In film, it is the photography of the mind."

Solution #1 — Question and Answer Railroad Tracks (any topic)

Whether the shot is in the script or purely a director's choice, there is a reason for the shot. Chances are, that reason is related to what your character is supposed to be thinking about. If you have trouble determining the reason or what you should be thinking about, ask the director, "What am I thinking about here?" Select a question about that to get you started on your Question and Answer Railroad Tracks. Or, start off listening to the other character, your scene partner, in your usual way and stay alert to something the other character says that can provoke a secret question in your mind.

Solution #2 — Question and Answer Railroad Tracks (the past)

Look at what has previously happened just prior to the scene or moment you are about to play. Did your character see or hear something? Did she learn something? Whatever it is, improvise to yourself a first question springing from that, a question that will put you on your Question and Answer Railroad Tracks. Let's say your character finds something important. As the scene proceeds, or in the next scene, ask yourself, as the character, an appropriate question about the discovery: "How did that get here?" or "Who put that there?" Any question will do. Only you will ever know what the question is. After you improvise the question, improvise your character's answer, and off you go down your Question and Answer Railroad Tracks.

Solution #3 — Question and Answer Railroad Tracks (the future)

If nothing has happened just prior to the shot that provides you with goodies to think about, look to the future. Does your character know about something that is going to happen? Improvise your first question based on that knowledge—for example, "What can go wrong?"

Solution #4 — Question and Answer Railroad Tracks (the present)

If nothing has happened just prior to the shot and nothing is going to happen that your character knows about, look at the present. Is something going on somewhere else right now that concerns your character and that your character knows about—for example, a staff meeting is taking place about whether or not you will be fired? Improvise your first question based on that knowledge—for example, "What are they saying about me?"

Solution #5 — Question and Answer Railroad Tracks (a discovery)

If you, the script, or the director wants your thinking to include a discovery, an important idea that will advance the plot, then you know ahead of time that you will have to get to a question whose answer will be the important idea, or the question itself will be the important idea. The important idea becomes a stop on your railroad tracks that is preplanned. Knowing this ahead of time will guide you as you improvise the beginning questions and answers that will lead you to the important idea. Knowing you have to get to it is sufficient for you to improvise in the moment. When you get to the idea, don't muscle getting the idea; just authentically think of it after the question or answer that takes you there. It will probably be your last answer or question on these railroad tracks. If the director doesn't call "Cut," turn the idea into a new first question and get on new question and answer railroad tracks. The first set of tracks leads you to getting the idea, and the second set of tracks is about what you are going to do with that new idea. Q: "Who put this here?" A: "The butler put it here (new idea!), and that means he's a suspect." Begin new railroad tracks starting with, let's say, Q: "How am I going to catch him?" Stay on these new tracks until the director calls " Cut."

If you want to give the director an opportunity to stay on you longer than he anticipated, create another turn. A turn is created when you get off one set of railroad tracks and get on another set. For example, upon arriving at the new idea that the butler did it, you might then turn onto another set of tracks about catching him. Your acting, the thinking, becomes more dynamic and less likely to be cut in the editing room when there is greater distance between the two sets of tracks—in other words, when you make a wide turn. Making multiple turns also results in more dynamic thinking. If you stay on the same track for more than three questions and answers, you should assume the editor will cut away from you. For more on turns, see Railroad Track Turns, [p. 6].

WHEN YOU NEED TO

PLAY THE STORY

To "play the story" means you must have responses to each of the story points that involve your character. Go through the script and label all the story points. A story point is an event or dialogue that moves the plot along by raising the stakes, speeding it up, or taking it in a new direction. Label the story points with brief factual statements: "She finds the missing gun," "He learns he has cancer," "He tells her for the first time that he loves her." If you are unsure whether something is significant enough to be a story point, look at what follows it. If what follows is based on the fact that it occurred, it is a story point. In other words, without the story point occurring, there would be no reason for the text that follows it. Sometimes a character provides new information that only fills out the backstory and is not significant to what follows. That new information would not be a story point.

At each designated story point, decide how your character responds to it. The choice is up to you as the interpretive artist. You should interpret and play what you think the writer intended. You will find clues to the writer's intention in the dialogue, punctuation, syntax, and stage directions.

Keep in mind that while looking for clues, the better choice may not be anything your character actually says in response to the story point. For example, a story point occurs and your dialogue following it includes the line "I'm tired." Based on the other clues, you interpret that the character's response to the story point is "frustrated." Even though your dialogue says you're tired, you are playing "frustrated" when you say the line. Use the writer's clues to make your interpretive choices so that you're telling *that* story, not *a* story.

Your story point responses should make sense for your character. For example, they may depict advancement or regression on your character's arc or be consistent with your character's persona. In comedies, while staying with choices that make sense for your character, be open to surprising choices that can get a laugh. The one and only Mel Brooks says, "A story point laugh is worth its weight in gold." When you are rehearsing, performing, or shooting the scenes with story points, make sure you play your responses, and you will have "played the story."

Always look at your acting choices before the story point. What you are playing just prior to the story point should be something that sets up a dynamic change. As Mel Brooks says, "Without a valley, there is no peak."

★ Solution #1 — Play a Specific Emotion

After you have chosen an emotional response to the story point (let's continue with the example of frustration), designate the beginning and end of the beat where you will play your response. The beat will begin after the story point occurs and end when you switch to another choice. It's up to you how many lines you will be saying and listening to while frustrated. Play that frustrated beat by physicalizing the frustration. This solution requires no additional choices. How to physicalize an emotion is presented in Physicalizing an Emotion [p. 31].

Solution #2 — Actions

Play an action (verb) that will lead you to the desired story point response. Here are some examples. If the desired response is frustration, pick an action that will fail in pursuit of your objective. For a response of pleased, pick an action that will be pleasing to do or will lead to an outcome that pleases you. Keep in mind when choosing the action that not only should it lead you to your desired response, it should also be one that is meant to overcome the obstacle to what your character wants (the problem or objective).

Solution #3 — Adjustments

Another approach would be to add an adjustment to your action choice. If what the character is doing is called the action, how the character does the action is the adjustment and is frequently called an attitude. This adjustment or attitude choice is usually an adverb modifying your action verb—for example, "protect frantically." Let's say the story point is a failed attempt at saving something or someone, and your story point response is frustration. Playing the beat by protecting frantically, and failing, should take you to your selected choice—frustration.

WHEN YOU NEED TO

PLAY THE SUBTEXT

When you receive a note to play the subtext, it means the scene is flat. Your acting is making the scene be about nothing more than what you are doing and saying. Screenwriter William Goldman (*All the President's Men*, *Butch Cassidy and the Sundance Kid*, *The Princess Bride*) advises writers: "If all that's going on in your scenes is what's going on in your scenes, think about it a long time." One of the ways writers make a scene be about more than what the characters are saying and doing is by using subtext. The text of the scene is about one thing and the subtext, or unspoken acting, is about something else. There should be something going on for your character in addition to what you are doing and talking about. The subtext is what the character is concerned with and focused on regardless of what he is saying or doing. It influences what the character is doing and saying while remaining unspoken, which is why it adds dimension to the scene as the audience sees something the character isn't telling them.

Different kinds of subtext can be added, from the simple to the more significant.

Solution #1 — A Character's Secret

Have a secret, unknown to the other characters and the audience. It can be your character's secret or your own. A character's secret is better because it's grounded in your whole performance and may lead to surprising discoveries about your character or the script. A personal secret can suffice if you find it to be rich and stimulating. Regardless of whether you go personal or character, no one else will ever know your secret. Here are some examples: You or your character is having an affair with another character or cast member, a famous person, a person with a different sexual persuasion, or anyone who inspires your imagination. You or your character is going to Tahiti tonight. Your fly or your character's fly is intentionally open and you're not wearing underwear. You or your character has just murdered someone.

Christopher Walken talks about secrets he picks just to amuse himself: "I've played scenes pretending I was Elvis or Bugs Bunny or a U-boat commander. I just don't tell anybody." A smart actor determines what the tone (feeling, status, stakes) of the scene's subtext should be and picks a secret that will provide that same tone. When playing the scene, focusing on your secret will make you more interesting and provide a subtext.

While focusing on the secret, stay open to your body's spontaneous and physicalized response. Don't anticipate or pre-plan your response; discover it in the moment.

★ Solution #2 — Script Subtext

Did the writer intend the scene to have a specific and built-in subtext? Look at the given circumstances to find out. You are looking for an event in the script that is significant to your character and is not spoken about in this scene but is probably what your character has on her mind. The event may be personal, such as a marriage proposal or breakup, or it may be more public, such as a community, national, or international crisis or advancement. The event may have occurred prior to this scene. If it will occur later in the script, your character has to know it's going to happen for it to function as subtext in the scene. It may be happening during this scene, but elsewhere (again, your character would have to know about it for it to function as subtext).

In some scenes, what begins as subtext is later elevated into the text. The characters start talking about what has been on their minds. The director Mike Nichols referred to subtext as the "dead whale" in the scene. He was talking about unspoken tension between characters that, like the smell of a dead whale, becomes so great that they can no longer avoid talking about it.

You also have the freedom to change the built-in subtext to another subtext as long as it has the same tone. If the built-in subtext has to do with your character committing suicide after you exit the scene, you don't want to change it to running away to get married, but you could change it to some other sad or fearful event you won't talk about. And you could change the subtext for each take or performance, thereby guaranteeing spontaneity.

When using a built-in subtext from the script, you might find that the characters and situation don't inspire, stimulate, or resonate with you. Let's say the built-in subtext of a scene is that you are going to make love at the end of the scene and you don't like the actor playing your partner. For the subtext, you might pick a different partner, a real lover from your personal life, or even a fantasy lover, and focus on this person. It's your choice to explore a substitution. Nobody else needs to know about it. All you're concerned about is the effect it has on you and your inner life. The trick is to self-monitor the stakes. Look at how high or low the stakes are of the built-in subtext and make sure that your substitution is going to create similar stakes.

★ Solution #3 — Character Subtext

If the scene has no built-in subtext, you can add one by choosing your own event. For instance, suppose the scene is about a card game. The given circumstances are that four robbers (Lou,

Nick, Leon, and Harry) playing cards at a hideaway in scene 4 will rob a bank in scene 5. We've seen this scene in many gangster and cowboy movies. In playing scene 4, the robbery clearly has subtext potential. However, discussion of the robbery is part of the banter (text) of the card-playing scene, so the robbery can't be subtext. How can the characters employ subtext on their own that's not built into the script?

Let's say the actor playing Lou adds subtext to the scene by deciding that he doesn't trust Nick. The distrust is based on an imagined event from the past. He and Nick were on a previous heist, and Nick betrayed him in some fashion. The effect of focusing on this imagined event from the past, about which the audience knows nothing, is distrust of Nick. Nick could choose to add to the subtext of the scene that he wants Leon's girlfriend. For his subtext, Nick might choose an imagined event in the future, sex with Leon's girlfriend. Leon, for variety's sake and contrast, doesn't play any subtext. He's totally focused on the card game. Harry could add to the subtext by choosing to be very frightened by the whole situation. His fear can be based on an imagined event occurring in the present—his wife, child, or parent is undergoing an operation right now. With these subtext additions, three of the characters are thinking about and being influenced by something other than the card game.

Picture the scene I have just described compared to the scene without these choices, four thugs playing cards with banter. These subtexts add dimension without changing one word of dialogue or adding any time to the scene. The actors have way more to do, and the acting is all spontaneously improvised in front of the camera. You have given the director more options to choose from.

No matter how small the part, subtext can add dimension to your scene. In Hamlet, Fortinbras enters one minute before the end of the play in order to wind things up. He sees the bodies, says he's going to look into taking over the kingdom, praises Hamlet as a good guy, and tells the soldiers to clean up the mess. That's his text. A director might ask the actor to say his lines decisively, in contrast to Hamlet. But the actor might ask himself, "Is there a subtext opportunity?" He might discover an event in the past, present, or future that has subtext potential—for example, his coronation as king. He still says the same lines and does everything the director is asking him to do, but now his character, focusing on the subtext, displays a hint of ego, maybe even the slightest touch of pleasure at his good fortune. On the other hand, being a noble, Fortinbras might find it déclassé to feel self-satisfied when the entire royal family of Denmark bites the dust. Focusing on his coronation might instead produce a feeling of grimness as he anticipates the responsibility that awaits him.

Make choices that may be considered a part of the whole scene and not simple impositions for the sake of making your part bigger. While focusing on the subtext, stay open to your body's spontaneous and physicalized response.

★ Solution #4 — Moment to Moment Subtext

Sometimes getting the note to play the subtext is not so much about the subtext of the scene, but about enriching the inner life of the character, moment to moment. If that's the case, you don't need a built-in or made-up subtext. Instead, traveling at any time in any scene can give the sense that something else is going on.

Traveling is easily accomplished by pursuing Question and Answer Railroad Tracks [p. 3]. Traveling is a technique for discovering what's really on your character's mind in any moment of the scene when you don't have lines and are listening to other characters. It adds a subtextual dimension to your listening and then influences your own speaking when responding. You discover thoughts and feelings that you hadn't previously considered, discoveries you hadn't anticipated. Traveling puts you in the character's head, not the actor's head, allowing thoughts and feelings to happen spontaneously with the control of a craftsman. It is applying form to spontaneity. Anything you hear or see can become a springboard for traveling. For example, suppose you are Happy in the Biff and Happy scene from *Death of a Salesman,* and Biff starts his lines about being out west and how Happy should join him there. While he is speaking, you might start a question and answer railroad track with "What does Biff really want from me? or "What's wrong with Biff?" Maybe the question is "Why am I listening to him?" Whatever the questions or answers, whatever the railroad tracks, it's pure improvisational discovery for you into your character. Or you are in rehearsal or performance for the same scene, and you notice what Biff is wearing. You observe that Biff has a hole in his sock. You might start your traveling with the question, "Who's going to give a job to a man with a hole in his sock?" Regardless of where your traveling starts and goes, your feelings are going to follow your thoughts. Your character might discover that he is suspicious and jealous of his brother, or he might discover that he appreciates his brother more than he thought he did. These are more character-driven than text-driven issues.

Traveling gives the audience the perception that something else is going on. And it is. In scripted acting, you know what the other character is going to say. But if you focus on traveling while he says it, you will hear it spontaneously, from a new angle, which will enrich your character's inner life.

All Solutions

Playing the Subtext

When you have selected the subtext, it will be what you are concerned about and focused on while playing the scene, regardless of your lines and business. It should influence all you say and do in the scene. If it does, the audience can sense that there is something else going on. They want to know what it is and will pay closer attention. They like a mystery, even in a comedy. What's going to happen when Oscar comes home late and Felix's roast is burned, but Felix says nothing about it?

Exploring

As you focus on the subtext and its ramifications, stay very alert to exploring it from different angles so you don't hang out with one cliché or obvious feeling. Discover thoughts and feelings that you hadn't previously considered, discoveries you hadn't anticipated. Consider, for example, a scene where all the characters have the same subtext—they are co-workers and had an orgy together last night. The scene takes place the next day at the workplace, and there is no mention of the orgy in the dialogue. The scene might start with everybody focused on their subtext. They are happy, playful, and bawdy. As they each explore different angles of the subtext, some of them discover that maybe having that orgy wasn't such a great thing. Jealousy might come up for one of the married characters: "Has she been making love to my husband before last night's orgy? I'm starting to feel abandoned whenever he smiles at her." Someone else comes up with an STD issue: "Did he use protection? I really don't know him that well." No one anticipates these developments as they begin the scene that takes place the next day. All they anticipate is fun and bawdiness. The drama of the situation evolves out of some of them spontaneously discovering the dark side. Just as you can explore the text of a scene, you can explore the subtext.

Physicality

"Actions speak louder than words" is one of those wonderful adages that will always be relevant. What do your actions say? Do you sit down or flop into a chair? Do you bang the cabinet door closed or close it slowly? Are you grasping your drink nonchalantly or in a shaking manner with white knuckles? When what you are doing (the activity or business) is influenced by the subtext, actions are still more revealing than words. Wherever possible, *combine your subtext work with physicality.* It is no big deal to stand in front of a camera or an audience and think about the subtext (like Rodin's *The Thinker*). What is a big deal is to be able to think about the subtext while talking about something else. An even bigger deal is to think about the subtext while talking about something else and allowing your body to do an activity or business at the same time, thus reflecting what's going on inside. A great example is the opening scene in *Inglourious Basterds* where a Nazi officer, nicknamed the Jew Hunter and played by Christoph Waltz, is making inquiries of a French farmer in his house. The text is about the Nazi seeking information about the town's Jews. Waltz is using subtext based on a future event, the efficient and successful extermination of any Jews hiding in this house. Throughout the scene, he is busy: removing items from his briefcase (including a jar of ink from which he fills his fountain pen), perusing lists and making notes in his notebook, drinking a glass of milk, and filling and smoking his pipe. The farmer, played by Denis Ménochet, is also occupied with filling, lighting, and smoking his own pipe while focusing on his subtext, based on an event that is simultaneously happening elsewhere: Jews are hiding under the floorboards beneath them. The actors' business contributes greatly to revealing the Nazi's confidence and the farmer's fear. This scene is also an example of the subtext rising into the text when Waltz eventually gets around to offering the farmer a deal to escape punishment if he tells where the Jews are hiding. Focusing on your subtext—whether it's an event, a secret, or question-and-answer railroad tracks—will manifest in how you move your body, use objects, and react physically to other characters, all of which the audience sees and understands.

Character

Frequently, you will make character discoveries as a result of employing subtext. For example, you may discover that your character always sees the dark side of an event. This alerts you to the possibility that your character is pessimistic, depressed, or angry. You can then bring that discovery to your total character work, or it may open a door for a new approach to another scene elsewhere in the script.

Multiple Takes

In camera acting, once you have decided on an event (past, present, or future) as your subtext, you can consider alternate choices to have available for multiple takes. Each of these preselected choices would have the same tone and put you in the same frame of mind that you (and the director) are looking for. Let's say you're doing a scene in a film and want three subtext events in case the director does three takes. Take one, subtext/future: "I have a date with the woman of my dreams." Take two, subtext/future: "I'm going to win the Oscar." Take three, subtext/future: "I'm presenting my parents with a gift, a beautiful house at the beach." Notice how all three of those choices are happy future events. The dialogue and blocking remain the same for each take, and all three takes will come out with a happy undertone. You are newly improvising each take, thinking about a future event for the first time, which creates, by necessity, true spontaneity. And no one needs to know what you are doing. All the director sees is someone who is so spontaneous that there are subtle differences in each take. If the director wants to change the tone of your subtext from take to take, deliberately select different subtext events that have a different tone. For instance, using the above examples, instead of you winning the Oscar, your biggest competitor for roles has won it. Now your subtext is a past event and won't have a happy tone, but a jealous one.

Is Subtext Necessary?

Not all scenes require subtext work. It depends on the writer's intention and how she wrote the scene. Some scenes have to be about what they're about. A conflict scene has to be about the conflict. Still, in some conflict scenes, the textual conflict is based on a subtextual conflict. If you are working on a scene where the given circumstances do not provide a built-in subtext and you get a note to play the subtext, consider Solutions #1, #3, and #4.

WHEN YOU NEED TO

MAKE A MONOLOGUE COMPELLING

When your performance of a monologue is generic and not specific, it's not compelling for the audience. Perhaps the monologue includes a story from the character's past, and you are performing it with a wistful tone of nostalgia as you look over the audience's heads, as if there is a distant mountain behind them. As you gaze at the mountain, you vividly conjure up from the character's memory the details of the story and the feelings experienced at that time. Every line you say is full of warmth and gentle amusement at how wonderful that experience was. You are totally caught up in the memory. It doesn't have to be nostalgia. It might be a singular tone of anger, fear, or tragedy. Whatever your choice for how you feel about this story, you are doing the whole monologue in only one tone, without specificity or variety. By the end of the monologue, the audience is snoring, if they haven't gone out for popcorn.

★ Solution #1 — Sophisticated Approach, Writer's Intention (requires preparation time)

Reconsider your approach to the monologue. Instead of focusing on what your character wants, focus on what the writer wants. Playing your choice of the character's objective does not necessarily serve what the writer intended and does not fully take advantage of the text. Writers intend monologues to reveal something about the character in addition to what the character says. If you fail to structure your performance around this character revelation, the monologue may be ineffectual and drag the scene down. Therefore, an interpretive choice is needed so you know what you are to play. In order to understand how to make these choices and play them, see Monologues: Breakdown and Rehearsal [p. 67]; Umbrella Arc [p. 57]; Make the Exposition Compelling, Solution #1 [p. 116].

★ Solution #2 — Fast Approach, Emotion Arc or Switch (no preparation time required)

With no time to plan a new approach to the monologue, you will immediately make the monologue more compelling if you pick an emotion the character might be feeling during the monologue and intensify that emotion over the course of the monologue—in other words, arc it [see Emotion Arc, p. 51]. For example, let's take the aforementioned nostalgia-inducing monologue. If the character is telling a story from her past that she fondly remembers, she could start the monologue feeling pleased (at the memory) and, as the monologue proceeds, heighten her feelings of pleasure as she became, in escalating order, amused, cheerful, giddy, jubilant, elated, and joyous. None of these heightened intensity levels of happiness need to be preselected or attached to preselected beats. They are simply levels that might be found while improvising a happy arc.

Another quick approach is to divide the monologue into two to four beats (or more) of different emotions the character might be feeling during the monologue. Play those beats with your emotion choices by switching emotions [see Make a Sharp Transition from One Emotion to Another, p. 141].

With either approach, should the director find your choices don't work, you have shown him very specific choices that will enable him to point you in the direction of other emotion choices for the next take or rehearsal. "You don't like me getting angrier throughout? What would you like? I could do sad and get sadder? Fear with more and more frightened?" or "You don't like angry switching into sadness? What would you like? I could flip it and go from sad to angry? Choose different emotions? What would you like?"

Solution #3 — Basic and Traditional Approach, Problems and Actions

To address this note and make the monologue more compelling, get back to what your character wants! And don't forget the given circumstances for determining the monologue's context. Who else is in the scene with you? Why is everybody there? Who are you talking to? Do you want something from them? Why not? After making the choice of what your character wants, needs, or desires (the problem or objective), check to see what's in the way of your character getting what he or she wants. If nothing is in the way, you have made a bad choice of a problem. The drama comes from your character overcoming your obstacles. No obstacles, no drama. After finally arriving at a choice for your problem and identifying your obstacles, choose what you are going to do to overcome them. This choice is called your action, and it should be a verb, something you can do. The more active the verb, the better. Examples of strong action verbs include: demand, convince, impress, ridicule, warn. To sum up, you have gleaned the context of the monologue from the given circumstances and have made three choices: problem, obstacles, and action. As you perform the monologue, *focus on playing your action* in order to solve your problem. Perhaps you now have a greater appreciation for what Stella Adler famously proclaimed: "The talent is in the choices."

The longer the monologue, the more likely it should be broken up into sections or beats. Each beat is an opportunity for a different action verb choice. Each beat and verb choice is a different approach to solving the designated problem. Different approaches to getting what you want make for variety and heighten the audience's interest. The length of continuous text dedicated to one action choice determines the length of a single beat. Beats are not determined by the subject matter of the lines; a new subject does not automatically begin a new beat. Beat beginnings and endings are determined by what you are doing, not by what you're saying. In addition, beats do not have to begin or end at the beginning or end of a sentence. They can begin or end mid-sentence or even mid-word. The director Elia Kazan, in what became known as the Kazan Transition, would deliberately have an actor transition from one beat to another one line or one thought earlier than where the transition should obviously occur or was meant to occur. This approach made it easier to hold on to one emotion while making a transition to another and made the meaning more dramatic. In Paul Newman's words, the Kazan Transition "affects the pace because you don't have to stop to make the transition."

If you are doing the whole monologue with one action choice, then the whole monologue is one beat. If you are doing two action choices, each choice is one beat with a transition between them, three beats have three action choices with two transitions, etc. The number of beats in a monologue is your interpretive decision.

Solution #4 — Fast Approach, Actions (no preparation time required)

Apply a different approach to defining the beats or sections of the monologue. Instead of defining them according to behavior changes, that is, your actions, it's faster, if less effective, to define the beats by subject changes because it takes less time to define the beats. Every time the subject of what you are talking about changes, start a new beat. Select a different action for each beat. Play your actions.

Solution #5 — Corrective and Traditional Approach, Super-Objective

Your monologue might not be working because you have not connected your approach to your *super-objective*. You may have been diligent in choosing and playing an action during the monologue that makes sense to you for this moment in the scene, but your choice is limited by being appropriate to only this moment in the scene. It is as if you have forgotten what your character really wants, needs, or desires for the entire script—the super-objective. What is the ultimate goal that dictates everything in the script relating to your character? In most scripts, this goal is fulfilled by the end of the story if the character is a good guy and thwarted if the character is a bad guy. Sometimes, a good guy's goal is thwarted at the end of the script, as in tragedies and even some comedies. Occasionally, the goal changes toward the end of the story, and the new goal is either attained or thwarted.

Review your choices for the monologue to see if they are in service of what you want in the scene and also in service of attaining your super-objective.

Ask yourself how the monologue relates to your super-objective and how your super-objective affects the monologue. Keep in mind that you are serving two functions simultaneously: playing an action for this moment in the script and fulfilling your super-objective.

Doing this review replenishes what is really going on for your character and may result in some new choices for the monologue. If nothing else, it will remind you of why you are there and what's going on for you throughout the entire script—the connective thread. If you make changes as a result of this review, you will add a new dimension to the monologue that should make it more compelling. Everything your character does and says is, in some way, influenced by your super-objective.

All Solutions

Regardless of the solution you employ, for longer monologues it helps if you think of your monologue as an entire script. It should have a beginning, middle, and end. It should have an idea, your interpretive choice, that you build, develop, and finish. At the end, you're at a place different from where you began. The journey from the beginning to the end is what makes it compelling. That is how Stephen Sondheim, as taught to him by Oscar Hammerstein II, approached a song (a song is a monologue plus music). In a monologue, your acting choices are the music.

WHEN YOU NEED TO

MAKE THE EXPOSITION COMPELLING

Some writers, including Christopher McQuarrie (*The Usual Suspects*, *Top Gun: Maverick*), believe that exposition should be revealed during character conflict in order to avoid boring the audience. As McQuarrie puts it, "Information is the death of emotion." But it doesn't have to be so.

If your character is tasked with providing background information, or exposition, consider why you are saying it and how you feel while saying it. Why is your character sharing this information with the other character(s) and the audience at this time? We know the exposition is there in order to make the plot or a character's arc or backstory more understandable. Those are the writer's reasons for including the exposition, not the character's reason for saying it.

Finding the character's reason starts with interpreting the context around this exposition. Is the exposition part of a conflict, confession, memory, warning, or something else? Make that interpretive choice. The clues to an effective choice are in the script. Start with the given circumstances leading up to the exposition. What is happening now? Who's involved? Where are you? At what point in the story is the exposition delivered? Is the exposition incited by an event or dialogue? Next, working in your script, exclude (~~strike out~~) the factual information in the exposition lines. What do the remaining words reveal about what the character is going through? In addition to what the character says, how does he say it? Consider syntax, for example: Why has the character's language, all of a sudden, become so formal? Or punctuation, there's a lot of exclamation marks! Or stage directions, such as emotional descriptions. Does the writer want the audience and other characters to see your character experiencing a particular emotion or going through some emotional or behavioral transition? For example, while speaking the expository dialogue, is your character feeling guilty, coming back from defeat, feeling abandoned, or excited about teaching or learning something? Or has the writer put the exposition where it is to show your character using it in an attempt to get what he wants? Script writers are taught that exposition should be ammunition, or they should cut it.

As long as you say the lines, regardless of how you say them, everyone will hear the information. Your job is to say the lines in a compelling fashion. Exposition becomes compelling and not just a recitation of dry information when your character delivers the lines as part of a larger context.

★ Solution #1 — Character Revelation

Whether the exposition is in the form of a monologue or dialogue, assume that the writer is also revealing something about the character. No matter what choice you make about this character revelation, we are still going to hear the information. This solution requires an ability to physicalize the emotion choices [see Physicalizing an Emotion, p. 31] or to play emotion arcs [see Emotion Arc, p. 51].

Step #1: Do the interpretive process outlined earlier in this entry leading to a choice for why the character is saying these lines and how he feels while saying them. Your choice may be purely an emotional choice. For example, your character is angry and is getting back at the other character by telling him information that will hurt him. Another kind of choice indicates a movement or direction for the character; examples include Coming Back from Defeat, a Loss of Illusion, a Celebration of Power. A third kind of choice might be feelings that are more complicated than a single, pure emotion; examples include denial, abandonment, betrayal, inundation, self-pity, excitement of learning or teaching. In order to understand how to make these choices and play them, see Monologues: Breakdown and Rehearsal [p. 67]; Umbrella Arc [p. 57].

Step #2: Let's use two examples: anger and coming back from defeat. For anger, mark the beginning of the beat where, in your interpretation, any hint of anger first appears. Mark the end of the beat where the anger stops. For coming back from defeat, start the beat where the character is feeling defeated or low. To find the end of the beat, look in the dialogue and stage directions for the moment in the script when the character has recovered from or moved past the feeling of defeat and now feels strong and perhaps victorious. The beat follows your character on a journey. Your exposition lines are said during this journey. I call this journey an umbrella arc. For more information on umbrella arcs and how to select and play them, see Umbrella Arc [p. 57]. Sample umbrella arcs and their breakdowns are found in Appendix A.

Step #3: You now have what may be a long beat and need to see if it should be subdivided into multiple beats. When dealing with a single emotion, you're unlikely to need multiple beats. However, if, over the course of the beat, the emotion intensifies or could intensify, you have two options. You can subdivide the beat into smaller beats that build in intensity. With anger, for example, the beats might be (1) frustration, (2) annoyance, (3) anger, (4) rage. Or you can provide the anger intensification, without making new beats, through your acting choice—by improvising an emotion arc [see Emotion Arc, p. 51]. If, over the course of the beat, the anger does not intensify, the beat can be characterized as an emotion plateau, not an arc.

If your long beat is an umbrella arc, you will need to subdivide the beat into beats of the emotions that fulfill that umbrella arc. This task is covered in Umbrella Arc [p. 57].

Step #4: Play the choices. *Rehearse if possible.* If the exposition is contained in a single beat of one emotion, rehearse that beat by physicalizing the selected emotion and focus on maintaining the physicalization as you say the lines. No attention should be paid to line readings, only the continued physicalization of the emotion. If you do that, however you say the lines will serve your purpose, and your body, mind, and voice will be free to make discoveries every time you run it. Consider it an improvisation where you explore playing that beat with that emotion and the scripted dialogue. What you are accomplishing with any rehearsals is practicing and improving your ability to stay focused on physicalizing the emotion while you say the text.

If you determine the beat should have a rising dynamic and you want to do an emotion arc, rehearse it first in the manner I have just described. Then rehearse it while focusing on intensifying the physicalization. You will know you have it when you never go backwards on the arc due to diminishing the physicalization. While arc climbing, it is okay if there are sections where you plateau in intensity and then resume climbing, but you never want any backing down (diminishing the intensity).

For an umbrella arc, you don't have to remember all the beat choices, because you are only going to be rehearsing one beat at a time. You can check your script where you have written the beat choices to tell you what choice is next. The rehearsal process for the umbrella arc (dialogue or monologue) is shown in Monologues: Breakdown and Rehearsal, How to Rehearse [p. 73].

In addition to saying the expository information, your acting is now revealing what your character is feeling. The exposition beat(s) is now about not just the information, but also character development. That is what makes it compelling. If you use the process outlined above, you will have planned your approach and rehearsed it and can now feel free to forget it. Just go with it! Don't be surprised when your body does not forget and does only what you planned better and better and always with the quality of a first time—that is, spontaneously.

Solution #2 — Actions

Whether it's a monologue or dialogue, determine where the exposition begins and ends. Divide that section into one or more beats and assign a different action for each beat. Changing the action from beat to beat creates a more dynamic performance. Make sure that your action choices (verbs, the more active the better) for these beats serve the whole context surrounding the exposition. For example, if the context is that your character is coming back from defeat when she says the exposition, an appropriate action for one of the beats might be to celebrate. If your character is feeling betrayed, an appropriate action for one of the beats might be to suspect. For another beat, it might be to punish. As you make these choices, remember that your character is also using the exposition, the sharing of the information, to get what you have determined she wants or needs (the *objective*, *problem*, or *intention*). Do not choose "to inform" as an action, because you are already informing by just saying the lines. Let's get two for one. For instance, you can inform and at the same time celebrate, punish, chastise, warn, persuade, encourage, incite, complain, coax, tease, challenge, inspire, torture, or most action choices.

As you play your action choices, emotions arise, so use them! Take advantage of a very powerful tool to aid you in getting what you want. Go with the emotions, integrating them in service of playing your actions, instead of squelching them. There may be occasions when holding your emotions in or controlling them tightly will be your character's choice. Be careful you don't use that as an excuse for not going with them. It is important to know the difference. Holding the emotions back because you don't want the other characters to see you get emotional in this moment must serve the authenticity of your character. It does not include—and is entirely different from—holding back your desire for what your character wants or needs.

Solution #3 — Paint a Picture

With your acting, "paint a picture" of the information you are providing. See the event, procedure, or details you are describing in your mind's eye. Create an internal movie, photograph, or painting of the information just for yourself. Make it as detailed as possible. Then use the text to make sure the character(s) you are speaking to can envision everything you see...moment by moment, beat by beat. While painting a picture is a lesser choice than the previous solutions, it will also take no time at all to jump into. You either respond to the suggestion that you "paint a picture" or you don't.

WHEN YOU NEED TO

DO IT AGAIN JUST LIKE THAT

Getting this note can be very satisfying or befuddling. Sissy Spacek captures the problem perfectly: "Even after all this time, I always think of acting as like catching a moving train and sometimes you [catch] that train and it takes you away and oftentimes, the train hits you and runs you over. When a scene really played and a director would say, 'Okay, now let's do that again. Do just what you did.' And I'd think, 'What did I do?' Because you're having an out-of-body experience; when it's in the moment, it takes you away with it. You forget everything." Shirley Knight tells a story about playing Irina in *Three Sisters* on Broadway, with Geraldine Page playing Olga. After a performance, Shirley was despondent because she felt she hadn't done well. Geraldine said to her, "You know what happened, don't you? You liked what you did yesterday, so you tried to do it again—and that's absolute death." Achieving a carbon copy of the previous take is not likely. Heraclitus said, "No man ever steps in the same river twice, for it's not the same river and he's not the same man." The next take can be done close enough to what the director called "perfect." He might even think it's better. The trick is to know what to focus on that will take you to a similar performance.

Solution #1 — Review Choices

Your personal technique led you to choices you made in the "perfect take." Review these choices. Were you focused on your objective and playing an action? Were you physicalizing an emotion? Were you working off an image? Were you listening to a particular piece of music just before? Were you focused on being in the moment? Whatever your choices were, focus on them when you do the scene again. Do not try to remember how you handled this or that moment or how you said this or that line. You will end up in your head, self-conscious, and there will be no spontaneity. Besides, your muscles have a memory of their own. Anything you did in the "perfect" take that was special will, most likely, be retained. Other than paying attention and staying alert, muscle (kinesthetic) memory doesn't require the mind's participation, certainly not conscious remembering.

Solution #2 — Substitution

If you didn't make choices for your "perfect" take, apply a substitution as your choice for the next take. Select a person in your personal or professional life who has the same relationship status to you as the other character in your scene. During the take, imagine you are talking to this person. You can substitute another person for every additional take. Each take will have the spontaneity of the "perfect" one. Focusing on this substitution will divert you from your concern about giving the director a carbon copy of the previous take. In addition, there is still room for your muscle memory to kick in with what felt good or right about the "perfect" take.

Solution #3 — Don't Do It

When the director asks you to do it again just like the previous take, say "Okay," but, when action is called, approach this take with a game plan you prefer, rather than attempting a replication of the previous take. Use this solution only if you have a new approach to the shot in mind and are ready to do it. As I have previously pointed out, duplicating a previous take is extremely difficult. There are also other reasons not to try. One of the greatest English-speaking actors, Alec Guinness, called the great French actor Jeanne Moreau "the most interesting actress I know." He visited a television show she was filming, where she showed that his meticulous replications were deadening: "Watching her filming I knew she was right; every 'take' was slightly different...spontaneous and fresh." Frank Langella made a similar point when talking about shooting *Dave*, directed by Ivan Reitman: "Whenever Ivan would yell, 'Cut,' my whole take on it would be, okay, he's printing it, he likes it, let's see what else I can do. Not, as it used to be when I was a younger actor—how can I reproduce it? What I just did is in the camera. The lens got it. It's there forever. If Ivan wants take six, Ivan is going to print it up and put it in the movie. *But maybe on take nine, I might do something wildly, wonderfully different and free, that he never thought of, and I never thought of.*"

WHEN YOU NEED TO

DO A CONTRADICTORY OR CONTRASTING DIRECTION

Directions that have two seemingly opposite or contrasting components are usually about emotions and attitudes. For example, a director might say, "She is fierce yet gentle." Separate the two components so that one is about your character and the other is about the emotion your character is feeling—she has a fierce personality or attitude and is feeling gentle.

★ Solution #1 — Attitude Line + Emotion Physicalization

Take on an Attitude Line—in this example, "I'm fierce" [see Attitude Line Process, p. 13]. After it's fully embedded in your whole body, affecting your personality, stance, posture, how you walk, how you talk, and how you handle objects, hold on to your fierce attitude and add an emotion physicalization of "gentle" [see Physicalizing an Emotion, p. 31]. You now have a fierce attitude and are feeling gentle and can fulfill the direction "She is fierce yet gentle."

Solution #2 — Actions and Adjustments

Pick an action verb that carries the attitude. For example, from the above note, I might pick "demand" as the action for a fierce attitude. As you say your lines, play your action verb, "demand," and add an adverb (an adjustment) that expresses the contrasting part of the note—"gently." Now your action with an adjustment is "demand gently." You can now fulfill the direction "She is fierce yet gentle."

WHEN YOU NEED TO

DO THE DIRECTOR'S LINE READING

Some actors hate being given line readings, and others are grateful. If the director's line reading reveals a different attitude than you have been using, then it is not about capturing the exact line reading but taking on that attitude. It's more complicated when a different attitude is not the issue.

Solution #1 — Discover the Meaning

Try his line reading. Repeat it a few times. Repeat it a few more times and include some lines before and after this line. Stay open to discovering how the new line reading changes the meaning or intention of what you are saying. Discovering the meaning yourself is better than asking the director for it. Integrate any new understanding of the line's meaning or intention into your delivery of the new line reading. Your discoveries may also alert you to potential changes in the beat leading up to the line and the beat after the line. If you don't discover any new meaning arising from the new inflection, ask the director what the new line reading means and how it's different from what you were doing. Learn what you can and use it to deliver the new line reading with meaning and life.

★ Solution #2 — Gibberish

What if you have trouble even imitating the director's line reading and can't capture where the director wants the inflection? Try saying the line and a few lines before and after it in gibberish. Substitute gibberish words for the actual text, in other words, improvise a translation of the English words to gibberish. You may have to do it a few times to be comfortable with the gibberish. The actual gibberish words and sounds will change with each pass. After a few passes in gibberish, run that part of the scene again in English and go with it in the moment without attempting to capture the requested line reading. Your body learned something about that part of the scene during the gibberish passes. Now you have to get out of the body's way and let it tell you how it wants to play those moments, including the line reading. Your brain will not have learned how to play those moments, but your body will. Your body's muscle memory from the gibberish will know what to do when you return to English. You may not capture the requested line reading; you may come up with a line reading you haven't done before. However, this post-gibberish line reading will have more truthfulness, confidence, and presence, thereby heightening the communication. The gibberish allows you to experience bringing your body into your voice while letting go of the effort and anxiety of producing a specific line reading. The director should be happy with this line reading, even if it's different from the line reading he provided to you.

IX

EMOTIONS

George Abbott was the undisputed dean of Broadway directors. He won six Tony Awards and the Pulitzer Prize and was honored by the Kennedy Center in 1982. Mr. Abbott relates how his drama professor at Harvard, G. P. Baker, the founder of the Yale School of Drama, hammered repeatedly on the importance of emotion in acting: "Get the greatest given emotional result from the given scene." Mimi Leder, prolific television and film director, hits the nail on the head: "I am most interested in what the character is feeling. I use my camera to emphasize those moments."

Playing specific emotions on cue can be very challenging. The challenge is heightened when you consider that many actors don't like to be told what emotion to play. Some actors are prone to denigrating a director's note for a specific emotion choice as a "result direction." I believe they feel that, as long as they play a good choice of an action, whatever emotion spontaneously emerges will be the right one for the scene. The situation isn't helped by how often these action-induced emotions, regardless of how authentic they may be, fail to fulfill the writer's intention for the emotional life of the character. An actor's technique is expanded when he has the ability to spontaneously play any emotion on cue, including the ability to interpret and play the emotion the writer intended.

[Reminder: Many of the solutions throughout the book involve the **Secret Magic Stuff** that I find to be most effective with the quickest results. Those solutions are highlighted by a star ★.]

WHEN YOU NEED TO

PLAY A SPECIFIC EMOTION

Let's skip over all the reasons your acting teacher said you shouldn't play a predetermined emotion. This is not the place to get into a theoretical discussion. Besides, we're losing the light!

It's not helpful if you are baffled as to why the director wants this emotion choice. Consider why your character might feel this emotion. Can you find an explanation or justification for it? If, after this consideration, you still don't know why, ask the director. Understanding this emotion choice puts it into context and makes whatever solution you use more accessible.

When working on a TV series, you might be asked to play a specific emotion because the production team has addressed what the character should be feeling, and the director is asking you for that choice. David E. Kelley, one of the most successful producer/writers in television (*L.A. Law, Doogie Howser, M.D., Chicago Hope, Ally McBeal, The Practice, Boston Legal, Big Little Lies*) has staff meetings on this subject. His team developed the "tone meeting," a formal opportunity for Kelley to systematically verbalize his written intents—for example, he might explain what emotional "color" for each of the leads in *Big Little Lies* he is going for in a scene. Mimi Leder, who has directed movies and over 100 television series episodes (*L.A. Law, ER, The Morning Show*), explains: "We make the choices in the writing and directing, and they [the actors] make the choices as to how big to go, or how small to go."

The first two solutions employ secret magic stuff, and then we get to more traditional approaches.

★ Solution #1 — Physicalize the Emotion

Here is an approach that requires no rehearsal time and about 30 seconds max for preparation. It can be done immediately after choosing which emotion you want to play or receiving the director's note to play any specific emotion. Directors love actors who can fulfill emotion notes with immediacy. In a rehearsal, you will be able try out different emotion choices for any part of any scene very quickly. You will also have the ability to shoot multiple takes with a different emotion for each take with only 30 seconds between takes. In addition, physicalizing an emotion heightens the actor's involvement in the moment and in the world of the performance while avoiding the isolation of an imagined world of memories, substitutions, and as-ifs.

Learning the mechanics will require doing a few exercises and a little practice. You will then be able to do it for the rest of your career. It's like riding a bike; once you learn it, you never forget how to do it. You can play any emotion or attitude that you, the director, or writer requires with hardly any time at all for preparation. Multiple takes of the same emotion choice will not be exactly alike, but they will all fit into a disciplined range.

To learn physicalizing an emotion, please go to Physicalizing an Emotion [p. 31].

★ Solution #2 — Attitude Line

If the director (or you) wants a specific feeling but can only describe it with phrases and sentences, rather than in one word, listen carefully to the description and discern that there is a prominent attitude running through the description. Name that attitude and then turn it into an Attitude Line. While attitude lines are primarily a character-building tool, they can also be used to help you through a speech, beat, or scene calling for a specific emotion or attitude. For an explanation of what an attitude line is and how to pick one, see Quickly Change to Director's Vision of the Character [p. 191]. To take on that attitude, see the simple process detailed in Attitude Line Process [p. 13].

Solution #3 — Affective or Emotional Memory

If you can identify a real-life situation from your past in which you experienced the required emotion, you can use that memory as a springboard to feeling it now. You will need to remember some details of the original experience. Re-create the original situation in your mind to the extent that you feel like you are having the experience again. If you get that far in the process, there is a good chance you will feel the same or a similar emotion now.

Here is an example of the process. Let's say the director wants you to be angry at another character at a particular moment. To start, think of a time when you were really angry with someone and confronted him or her. That's the memory you will work with.

After selecting the memory and before starting the process, it's very important to relax your body. Let all tension float away. If you have a favorite relaxation process, use it. Then, in your mind's eye, see the location where you had the encounter with that person. See all the large structures and objects. See the furniture. See the small objects. Notice the lighting. Now see all the colors. See the whole location a hundred times more clearly. See any people there. See how they are dressed. See what they're doing. See yourself there doing whatever you were doing at that moment. Hear any sounds that you remember from that moment. See the person who aroused your anger. If you remember, see how he or she is dressed. Hear the gist and attitude of whatever was said to you at the time. By now, the feeling of anger should be emerging in your body. Allow your body to go with it and avoid any resistance to that feeling. Whatever you feel, go with it. Let the feeling grow. Stay aware of how your body is responding to the process. Notice if your body is tensing or relaxing. How about your breathing? Is it different? How? Is your facial expression changing? How about your posture? To the best of your ability, observe the details of what's going on with your body while maintaining this rising feeling of anger. If taking notice of your physical responses distracts from the power of the memory, stay with the memory and let go of the self-observation. Or not. If you can self-observe, you will benefit in the future by increasing your ability to spontaneously create the feeling when you are in the moment during a performance or in take after take.

While you are feeling the anger, run the part of the scene where you or the director wants you to be angry. Let go of whatever your previous acting choices had been and stay focused on your memory as much as you need to in order to fuel the anger. You may find that at this point you don't need the memory at all.

Ideally, you should repeat this process three times to ensure its workability. As you repeat it, you should notice the angry feeling emerging more quickly each time. With practice, just starting to replay the memory will trigger and release the feeling. When repeating the process, you may notice that there is one particular detail of the memory that serves as the trigger for the emotion. As you continue with repetitions of the process, see how quickly you can get to that detail. Can you start with that detail and still release the emotion? After a few times, you may not even need a trigger.

On a shooting set, unless there is time for a break, affective or emotional memories will be of minimal help if the director gives the note to do it "angry" (or whatever emotion he picks) and expects you to jump into the next take. On the other hand, if you have had time to prepare and practice the memory and you have found the triggering detail, that's all you need. If you have not found a trigger, there is a shortcut that will speed up access to the feeling and serve you well when you need the feeling on multiple takes or set-ups. Instead of re-creating the memory, just have your body take on the physical details you were noticing the first time you did the process. Your body's response to the anger you felt probably included head-to-toes tension, leaning slightly forward, closing your mouth and clenching your teeth, partly closing your eyes, and breathing through the nose. If you do these physicalizations, your brain will recognize what you're doing as what the body does when it is feeling anger and release that feeling. Heightening or lessening any of these physicalizations is easy, natural, and integral to adjusting the intensity of the feeling. For example, your teeth can just touch and not clench, or your eyes might narrow less. You can also control the amount, or degree, of tension throughout your body. The physicalization is easily and fully enhanced by the contextual detail of the scene and will serve you well when you feel the power of the memory is fading.

You do not want to be doing the memory exercise during a take or a performance because it takes you away from the world of the scene. If you have prepared with the exercise, your preparation will prompt the spontaneous introduction of the emotion when needed. If not, a quick flash on your trigger should suffice. When physicalizing, you don't have to be concerned about "indicating" or performing some generalized or cliché form of the emotion if you physicalize all parts of your body while listening, saying your lines, and doing any business. If the affective or emotional memory works for you, consider for easy and timely access creating a catalogue of memories and triggers for multiple emotions. Stay alert to the necessity for preparation time and the possibility that your choices do not lead you to the required emotion. If they do not, more time is needed for adjusting your choices. Whether on camera or stage, consider what Academy Award-winning actor Kathy Bates has to say about emotional memories: "I've found, for me personally, that that can make the work self-indulgent, and that it can be psychologically harmful to use. Because if you continually finger those emotional memories in yourself, you can distort your relationship to them."

Solution #4 — Substitution or As-If

Is there someone from your life, in the present or past, whose presence would trigger the required emotion? If you think playing the scene opposite that person instead of the other character will provoke the required emotion, do a substitution, or as-if. Let's say the scene is about your character failing to discern that he is patronizing another character. When the other character points this out, the director wants you to feel embarrassed. When you attempt to feel embarrassed, for whatever reason, the director says that it's coming out as shame, a very heavy choice. It communicates that your character feels he has failed to live up to his own expectations and that he feels terrible about it. The director continues, telling you it's important that your character not have the depth to achieve this self-awareness. Your character should only be embarrassed, like it's nothing, like being seen with your fly open or accidentally farting in public. Embarrassment is lighter than shame. You understand the director's point, but you don't know what will take you there.

What to do? Is there someone who provokes the light kind of embarrassment the director is talking about? Someone who would make you feel awkward or self-conscious, in a light way? It could be someone in your life or even someone you have never met, a glamorous movie or rock star. Play the scene and substitute in your mind that person for the character you are playing the scene with, *as if* you are playing the scene with that person. This was exactly what Dustin Hoffman did when playing Benjamin in *The Graduate.* In the scene where he checks into the hotel for his tryst with Mrs. Robinson, he was struggling with the delicate distinction between embarrassment and shame. Mike Nichols, the director, led him to remember a situation from his past that caused him embarrassment—trying to buy condoms as a teenager. Nichols then told him to substitute a female pharmacist for Buck Henry, who played the hotel desk clerk. The scene then became one of the most memorable in that classic film. An as-if could be any situation in which, in your mind, you swap out something in the scene with something that isn't, in order to play it better. Character substitution is one kind of as-if.

While waiting for "Action" to be called, start visualizing the person you are substituting. The more detailed the visualization, the better. Keep narrowing the visualization—see their whole body, then the face, the nose, lips, eyes. Convince yourself you are playing the scene with this person. Transfer the face of this person onto the face of the actor you are playing the scene with. As the scene progresses, go with the feeling that arises. Let the feeling grow and dictate how you are playing the scene, especially line readings. Don't try to hold on to your previous acting choices.

Solution #5 — As-If

Instead of using real parts of your life as buttons to trigger the desired emotion, you can rely completely on your imagination. Ask yourself what situation might provoke the required emotion. The closer the imagined situation is to the designated scene, the better. Let's say, for example, you or your director want your character to feel guilty. In the scene, your character's marital partner is confronting you with the fact that he or she knows you have been cheating. In rehearsal or after a take, the director says you are playing the scene defensively, and he wants you to play it feeling guilty. He says defensiveness is the avoidance of guilt and wants your character to accept it and feel it. And there is nothing in your own life to equal this marital situation. You have never been married or even had a relationship that approximates it. What to do?

Ask yourself if there is something you can imagine that captures the essence of this situation and has meaning for you. In this case, consider what it would be like to be caught by someone close to you doing something you were not supposed to do and thereby letting this person down. What do others expect you not to do? How about stealing? No one who knows you would expect you to be a thief. Getting caught cheating on a spouse is as if you were caught red-handed with stolen goods. As you get closer to selecting the situation you are going to imagine, pay attention to matching the stakes involved. Does stealing compare to marital cheating? Perhaps it depends on what you steal and who catches you. In the script, your wife catches you cheating, but that isn't working for you. Who would be as important as a wife and would be reasonable to imagine? Your mother. The imagined event gets clearer. Your wife catching you cheating would be as if your mother caught you in the act of stealing money from where she has hidden it. You can imagine it clearly and vividly.

Imagine it. To start, it's very important to relax your body. Let all tension float away. If you have a favorite relaxation process, use it. Then imagine yourself in the location where the money is hidden. See the location from within, not from the outside. You are there. See the furniture. See the large objects. See the small objects. Notice the lighting. Now see all the colors. See the whole location a hundred times more clearly. See where the money is. Imagine taking it. As you are counting it, look up and see your mother coming in. See how she is dressed. See her face. Hear the gist of whatever you imagine she says to you. By now, the feeling of guilt should be emerging in your body. Allow your body to go with it. Let the feeling grow. Stay aware of how your body is responding to the process. Notice if your body is tensing or relaxing. How about your breathing? Is it different? How? Is your facial expression changing? How about your posture? To the best of your ability, without losing this feeling of guilt, observe the details of what's going on with your body, how it's physically responding to the feeling.

While you are feeling the guilt, let go of the image of the as-if situation and also your previous acting choices. Run the part of the scene in which the director wants you to feel guilty, focusing on maintaining your guilt feeling. If, in the middle of the scene, you feel the emotion or the physical expression of the emotion slipping, or if you need to refresh it for multiple takes, you don't need to re-visualize the as-if. Just physicalize those body details you noticed earlier in the process. You were probably relaxing your body with a sense of collapsing, drooping your shoulders, glancing downwards, opening your mouth slightly with the corners pulling down. Your brain will associate these details with feeling guilty and heighten that feeling. You have the ability to adjust the extent of any part of the physicalization; it comes naturally within the context of the scene. Maybe your shoulders droop less or more, or your mouth doesn't open. Adjusting the extent of the physicalization is integral to adjusting the intensity of the feeling. The physicalization process will serve you well when you feel the power of the as-if fading. In addition, the physicalization will be in character and in the here and now, as opposed to your imagination. It will heighten your spontaneous involvement with the other characters and the circumstances of the scene, adding contextual detail.

There are many different variations of as-if. It can be as simple as imagining a situation that will provoke the desired emotion. Need to be afraid? It's as if there is a deadly snake advancing toward you and you can't move. Need to be happy? It's as if you just won an Oscar. It's best not to do your as-if during a take or a performance because it takes you away from the world of the scene. If you have prepared with the exercise, your preparation will prompt the spontaneous introduction of the emotion.

Should you use the physicalization refresher, physicalize all parts of your body while listening, saying your lines, and doing any business. Applying physicalization to your object handling is very important. Are you doing the business and handling any props with frightened, happy, sad, or angry hands? Don't forget the rest of the body! If most of your body is not physicalizing the emotion—for example, if only your hands are angrily gesticulating or throwing clothes into the suitcase—you are only indicating. Not good.

WHEN YOU NEED TO

MAKE A SHARP TRANSITION FROM ONE EMOTION TO ANOTHER

When a character suddenly changes from one emotion to another, it is dynamic, compelling to watch, and never left on the cutting room floor. As in real life, scripted characters' emotions are short-lived and transitory.

Regardless of how you define your beats in a scene, if a character is in a scene for more than one beat, that character usually goes through emotional changes (or should). The transition moment, or turning point, may be improvised or planned.

★ Solution #1 — Emotion Switch

Using an **Emotion Switch** requires no guesswork anticipating what emotions might emerge with different objective and action choices. It's easy to do with no rehearsal, though running it one or two times first will be valuable in terms of confidence and dexterity. It does require an ability to physicalize an emotion [see Physicalizing an Emotion, p. 31].

Break down the speech, beat, or scene into two sections, or beats, divided by the transition cue. The beat prior to that turning point will be emotion #1 and the beat following will be emotion #2. To make the emotion choices for the two beats, you have to interpret what you think the writer intended the character to be feeling during these beats. Look at the character's lines leading into the turning point and interpret what you think the writer intended the character to be feeling when saying these lines. Make that emotion choice for beat #1. Then back up in the dialogue from the turning point to where you interpret that the character first has that feeling, which will be the beginning of beat #1. Next, determine the emotion choice for beat #2 by interpreting what you think the writer intended the character to be feeling when saying the lines immediately following the transition. Determine the ending of beat #2 by going forward in the dialogue from the turning point to where you interpret the writer intends for the character to stop having that feeling.

If there is time to rehearse: Rehearse one beat at a time. Do the first beat and physicalize the emotion choice [Physicalizing an Emotion, p. 31]. Repeat the beat as many times as necessary until you are thoroughly physicalizing the emotion and playing it fully. Do the second beat in the same way. When you are confident with the second beat, do your first run-through of the two beats. For the run-through, improvise, without any hesitation, the turning point between the beats, making sure to physicalize emotion #2 as you start the second beat. Do the transition in rhythm—no hesitations for decision making or for any reason. Continue to focus on physicalizing emotion #2 until the beat ends. You are now doing an emotion switch. The switch must be total and immediate, not gradual, to fulfill the director's note to make a sharp transition from one emotion to another. For the sake of practicing the Emotion Switch, do a few run-throughs of both beats together prior to shooting.

It's important that you treat each run-through of the individual beats and the run-throughs of both beats together as an opportunity to practice physicalizing the emotions. While you are always saying the scripted lines of either beat with its emotion choice, the emotion's intensity and line readings might come out a little different each time, and you should be open to that possibility. Being open to it coming out somewhat different every time is not the same thing as deliberately making changes, which should not be your focus.

If there is no time to rehearse: For camera acting, there will be very little or no time for rehearsing on the set. Treat the first take as if it's a rehearsal for you to do your Emotion Switch. Physicalize emotion choice #1. Spontaneously handle the turning point by changing the physicalization to the physicalization of emotion #2. If the director calls for multiple takes, treat each take as an opportunity to practice the same Emotion Switch. Each take should have you physicalizing the same emotions with room for them to come out a little different each time. See the previous paragraph's notes about run-throughs for further explanation. As long as you fully physicalize with your whole body, with or without business, any dialogue you have will be infused with the emotion.

Acting is not about what you say. It's about what you do with the words you say, what the character is going through emotionally, the behavior of the character. Use the text (sentence meanings, word choices or syntax, punctuation, stage directions, and the given circumstances) to lead you to interpretive choices and then play those choices spontaneously while you say the text. In this approach, the length of a beat is determined by an emotion choice. When the emotion changes, the beat changes. No attention is paid to emotion #2 until somewhere during the turning point. If the director makes the emotion choices for you, other than understanding the context for her choices, your job is easier because you don't have to do the interpretive breakdown to arrive at the choices. On the other hand, if you disagree with the director's choices and want to suggest otherwise, you can use your breakdown to support your suggestion.

★ Solution #2 — Attitude Line Reading Switch

A sudden change in a character's emotions may also be achieved by changing the line reading for your character's attitude line [Attitude Lines: Process and Archetypes, p. 9]. Find a new line reading for your attitude line that captures the desired emotion. For example, if the attitude line is "I give up" and you have been saying it to yourself with a defeated line reading and you want a sharp transition to happy, explore a line reading that is happy, for example, "I give up (I'm free now!)." At the desired transition point, refresh your attitude line with the new attitude line reading and let your body respond immediately as you commence your dialogue.

Solution #3 — Changing Actions

Using a traditional approach with objectives (or problems) and actions requires breaking down the scene and rehearsing your choices. Break down the scene (or beat) into two sections, or beats, divided by the cue where you or the director want the transition. Determine the beginning of the first beat that ends at the transition by picking your *action* (verb) for that beat and determining where you start playing that action. Where you start will be the beginning of the first beat. The second beat starts at the transition cue. Pick the action you will play at the start of this beat and end the beat where the text suggests you stop playing that action. Where you stop will be the end of the second beat.

Pay attention as to whether or not the objective changes from the first beat to the second because it will influence your action choice for the second beat. Whether the objective changes or not, you now have two beats, each with a beginning and an end and their own verb choice, and the transition cue between them. When determining your action choices, pick actions that you think will produce the desired emotions for each beat. Linking an emotion to an action requires some interpretation and guesswork. Time for rehearsing may be necessary to confirm that you are arriving at the desired emotions. If not, change your choices, or you can experiment, taking advantage of how the actions are stimulating your emotions and going with it while guiding the arising emotion in the direction of the desired emotion. While you are guiding, stay out of your own way. Avoid self-doubts or judgments of how well or poorly you are doing it. You are in the moment, and all you can do is your best. You might even catch the wave, and it will be effortless.

To rehearse, follow the rehearsal procedure in Solution #1, substituting playing your action for physicalizing the emotion.

Solution #4 — Changing Adjustments

As in Solution #2, you are using objective and action choices, but you will not change your action choice. Instead, you play one action choice for the length of the speech, beat, or scene, and, at the turning point, you will change how you perform the action by changing the adjustment adverb. For example, if the action is to warn, you could warn gently and, at the turning point, transition into warning forcefully.

Select your objective and action choice for the length of the speech, beat, or scene, and subdivide that material into two sections (beats) divided by the transition cue, each with a different adverb. If, for example, your objective is "I want her to go away" and your action choice is "to belittle," the two beats might be labeled and played as "to belittle charmingly" and "to belittle viciously."

Rehearse one beat at a time. When you are confident that you have the first beat and you are fully playing the action and showing the emotion or attitude, do the second beat. When you are confident with the second beat, do your first run-through of the two beats and spontaneously handle the transition at the cue, keeping in mind the director wants a sharp transition. You will probably get it on the first run-through and be ready to go. If not, do multiple run-throughs until you have it. In the end, you will be making a sharp transition from, in this example, charming to vicious.

WHEN YOU NEED TO

INTENSIFY AN EMOTION INSTEAD OF FLATLINING

Flatlining—sustaining an emotion at the same intensity level for an entire beat or scene—can make the audience lose interest, whereas intensifying an emotion is almost always compelling. The director might say, "It would be great if you got more and more frightened as the scene goes on," or, "Get angrier and angrier throughout the speech." This kind of note speaks for itself. In terms of technique, the director wants an *emotion arc*, matching the emotion intensification to the length of the speech, beat, or scene. As you climb an emotion arc, other characters in the scene will respond accordingly, and the whole scene will climb its own arc, compelling the audience to become even more involved.

★ Solution #1 — Emotion Arc [no rehearsal time needed]

Doing an emotion arc is similar to playing a musical scale while considering how loud, how soft, how soon, how late. For example, the character's emotion might rise gradually to a frenzied crescendo.

Learning how to do an emotion arc will require a little practice, but you will then be able to do it for the rest of your career without having to re-learn the mechanics. It's like bike riding—once you learn to do it you have it for life. You can arc any emotion or feeling without time for preparation.

To learn how to do an emotion arc, please go to Emotion Arc [p. 51].

★ Solution #2 — Emotion Switches

This approach requires you to make a series of Emotion Switches within one emotional family to achieve the emotion arc.

Start by making a list of emotions that are in the same emotional family (anger, fear, happy, or sad) as the one the director wants you to arc. You can use the lists in the back of this book for guidance [see Appendix C, p. 272]. If the director wants you to get more and more frightened, your list might look like this: scared, cautious, aware, suspicious, nervous, concerned, anxious, frightened, apprehensive, terrified, alarmed, agitated, horrified. Rearrange the list from least intense to most intense: aware, concerned, suspicious, cautious, nervous, anxious, apprehensive, alarmed, agitated, scared, frightened, terrified, horrified. Divide the section you want to intensify into beats and label the beats with choices from the list. What would your character be feeling when saying the lines of each beat? Each beat should have a choice more intense than the previous choices. For example, let's say you are going to do the section you want to intensify in six beats. Your choices might be: (1) Cautious, (2) Nervous, (3) Apprehensive, (4) Scared, (5) Frightened, (6) Terrified.

If there is time to rehearse: You do not have to remember the beat choices, because you are only going to be rehearsing one beat at a time and can check your script to see your choice. You must be off book and know your lines cold. Physicalize the first beat choice using Physicalizing an Emotion [p. 31]. Run the first beat while physicalizing that emotion. Repeat the beat as many times as necessary until you are thoroughly physicalizing the selected emotion. Although you are rehearsing the scripted lines of that beat with the same emotion, it might come out a little different each time. You are never attempting to retain a favorite line reading. Your goal is to always play that emotion while being open to whatever differences come out in intensity, timing, or inflection changes.

When the first beat is done, work on the second beat with its emotion choice, approaching it the same way. When you are finished with the second beat and you are fully physicalizing the choice and the lines flow easily, do a run-through of the first two beats, improvising the turning point between them. You are now doing an Emotion Switch [Make a Sharp Transition from One Emotion to Another, p. 141]. Approach the third beat in the same thorough fashion as the first two beats. When you are accomplished in the third beat, do a run-through of the first three beats, spontaneously handling the turning points between them. Continue this process for every beat. The run-through after working on the last beat can be your final run-through of the whole scene. You have the opportunity, if time allows, for more run-throughs of the scene for practice. You are now ready to play the scene fulfilling the director's note to intensify the emotion throughout the scene.

If there is no time to rehearse: For camera acting, there will be very little or no time for rehearsing on the set. Solution #1 is preferable to solution #2, or you can do the above breakdown of the beats ahead of time. As the shot is being set up, look at your choice for the beat(s) that will be included in the shot. Play that choice by physicalizing it. If the shot covers material spanning more than one beat, you will have to remember the necessary choices and improvise the turning points between them as Emotion Switches. If the director calls for multiple takes of the same shot, treat each take as an improv even as you say the scripted lines with the same emotion choice, so that it may come out a little different each time. Other than very important moments with props or blocking, don't worry about matching. Experienced professionals are fond of quipping, "Matching is for pussies." As Elia Kazan said, "It's a gamble. But it's a better kind of trouble, though, than having a dead scene." Brent White (editor of *Ghostbusters*, *Arthur*, and *The Heat*, among others) opined about the challenge of editing mismatched shots: "Who cares? The performance is strongest in *that* cut!" This approach to editing was ingrained in him by one of his mentors, Dede Allen, who cut *Dog Day Afternoon*, *Serpico*, *The Hustler*, and *Bonnie and Clyde*. White contends that, in the audience, we "look at actors' eyes most of the time, so as long as they keep engaging, you're going to be connected to that person, and whatever happens elsewhere in the frame is less important."

Solution #3 — Changing Actions or Adjustments
Variation #1 — Actions

To intensify an emotion by changing actions, you first need to choose your objective or problem for the section you want to intensify and divide that section into beats with a different action for each beat. All the actions are attempts at overcoming your obstacle(s) and getting what you want. Each action should be more intense than the previous one, which will make each beat more intense. For example, let's say your objective in the scene is to get away from an intruder. The obstacle to your objective is that the intruder is big, tough, insistent, and menacing. The director wants you to become more and more frightened. You might choose to break down the scene into four beats, each with its own action, and each action is more intense than the previous beat's action— for example, (1) Distract, (2) Persuade, (3) Demand, (4) Escape. Playing the scene requires you move from one beat to the next because your actions are unsuccessful and, in this example, you feel the threat rising. These successive actions should produce rising fear. When choosing your actions, keep in mind that there is a difference between reality and fiction. Fiction has to make sense, so make sure that your action choices make sense for the situation.

Variation #2 — Adjustments

With this approach, you will play only one action for the length of the section you want to intensify and change *adjustments*—how you are performing your action choice. Adjustments, sometimes called *attitudes,* are usually adverbs modifying the action verb.

Select your objective and action choice for the section you want to intensify. Break down that section into beats with different adverbs of increasing intensity. If the director wants you to arc (intensify) fear and your objective is to get away from the intruder, and your action choice is to escape, each successive beat might be labeled: escape, (1) Cautiously, (2) Nervously or Apprehensively, (3) Fearfully, (4) Desperately. Playing your action, to escape, with these successive attitudes and respecting the given circumstances should produce rising fear.

Variation #1 and #2

Whether playing successive actions or one action with successive adjustments, the actor, aware of the director's note to become more and more frightened, takes advantage of how the action(s) and attitudes are stimulating his emotions by going with it and becoming more and more frightened.

WHEN YOU NEED TO

CRY

In *The Wild Duck,* Ibsen says we need to invent a life lie that allows us to go on with our lives. Destroy that life lie at the risk of destroying your life.

In most scenes in which a character cries, and in almost every monologue calling for crying, the character is experiencing the destruction of their life lie. This loss of illusion has an impact on the character comparable to the grief and devastation that follow the death of a loved one or a best friend. The character has lived a significant part of her life holding hands with this illusion and running her life in order to accommodate it, and now she is losing it, her best friend. She is confronted with a harsh truth about herself—her code of behavior, the way that she has been living her life, her guiding force, has been an illusion. She has been fooling herself. It's even worse because the character realizes no one made her adopt the lie she has been living. She alone is responsible for her own inauthenticity. The feeling provoked is not just sadness, but despair. No wonder the character cries.

It's important to know why your character cries, and it's easy to be distracted by the obvious reasons, such as a death, an abandonment, a betrayal, or a failure. While the crying may be triggered by one of these things, you should also consider that the obvious reason is also the catalyst for the loss of the life lie. Paradoxically, when the life lie is not a self-initiated path to inauthenticity, but a truth that only becomes a lie due to an unforeseen and extraordinary event, the loss of this kind of illusion is just as devastating. For example, if your character is faced with the death of a son or daughter, there is also a loss of an illusion—the child would outlive you. In almost every monologue with a stage direction calling for crying (and there are many of these monologues), underlying the triggering event is a loss of illusion.

In most cases, crying requires a combination of empathy and technical craft.

When faced with having to cry, after designating any obvious reasons for the crying, interpret the scene and articulate what illusion is being lost. What is the lie the character has to give up? It is important to identify and understand the specific loss of illusion because it will make it easier for you to identify with and understand the character's plight. It will stimulate your empathy for the character and put the crying in a context that has more meaning for you.

Knowing what illusion is being destroyed is important regardless of which acting solution you select as your approach. In fact, you may not need a tool, such as the solutions below, because you may discover you can just cry in the moment due to the empathy that accompanies being so focused on your character and what she is going through. Meryl Streep has spoken extensively on the power of empathy and acting: "Empathy is at the heart of the actor's art. In my work, it's the current that connects me and my actual pulse to a fictional character, in a made-up story. It allows me to feel pretend feelings and sorrows and imagined pain. And my nervous system is sympathetically wired, and it conducts that current to you sitting in the movie theatre…so that we all feel that it is happening to us at the same time."

Here are some examples of characters who lose their illusions in monologues containing the crying stage direction near the end of the speech. These selections are chosen to illustrate a wide range of lost illusions.

Kramer vs. Kramer—Joanna gives up the illusion that she is a good mother.

Three Sisters—Irina gives up the illusion that she is going to Moscow. Andre gives up the double illusions that he is happily married and successful.

Summer and Smoke—Alma gives up the illusion that John is her great and noble love.

A Raisin in the Sun—Walter gives up the illusion that he will be a great success and reward his family.

Truly, Madly, Deeply—Nina gives up the illusion that time will heal her grief.

Death of a Salesman—Linda gives up the illusion that Willy and she will live together happily in retirement.

Requiem for a Heavyweight—McClintock gives up the illusion that he was a star athlete.

The Goat, or Who Is Sylvia?—Stevie gives up the illusion that she has a good marriage based on mutual love.

The Seagull—Nina gives up the illusion that coming home will make everything okay.

The Cherry Orchard—Ranevskaya gives up the illusion that she will live in her home until her death.

Golden Boy—Lorna gives up the illusion that she will never fall in love again.

Side Man—Jonesy gives up the illusion that he will be a trumpet player for the rest of his life.

The following solutions utilize different approaches:

★ Solution #1 — Monologues — Physicalizing Loss of Illusion—Umbrella Arc

All the mechanics of this solution heighten your presence in the moment (as opposed to the isolation that may accompany the imagined world of memories, substitutions, and as-ifs). You are in the here and now of the scene. The whole loss of illusion monologue becomes very dynamic and compelling to watch because this approach choreographs the character's emotional journey with multiple emotions, not just sadness. It requires breaking down the monologue into choices and rehearsal.

Articulate the illusion. You are an interpretive artist playing this character, which requires that you understand how the triggering event is just the tip of the iceberg. What belief does the event destroy? Read backwards in the script from the moment of the stage direction to cry and identify where the beat begins. If the stage direction occurs in a monologue, the beat will usually start at the beginning of the monologue. Sometimes it will start a few lines earlier, in the dialogue that precedes the monologue. The beat will end at the end of the monologue. Label the entire beat—Umbrella Arc: Loss of Illusion [name the illusion]. Divide the beat into smaller beats or sub-beats of different feelings/emotions that a person goes through when experiencing a loss of illusion. Your choices should be based on your interpretation of what the character is feeling in each section of the monologue. The clues for making good choices can be found in the text of the monologue (sentence meanings, word choices or syntax, punctuation, stage directions) and the given circumstances.

What is the character feeling? Your choices shouldn't be based on repeating what the character says. They should be based on your interpretation of one or more of the clues in the monologue. Select your feelings/emotions from the following list. *It's very important that you label some, or all, of these sub-beats from the most common emotions accompanying loss of illusion, marked with an asterisk (*).*

Loss of Illusion emotions

anger *	misery	disgust
sadness *	fear	loneliness
guilt *	disbelief	isolation
embarrassment *	shame	frustration
confusion *	grief	bitterness
snobbery *	resentment	hopelessness
defensiveness *	regret	lostness
despair *	loss	

The final sub-beat where the crying usually occurs will be labeled either sadness or despair. Each of the other sub-beats gets its own label from the above list. To make these choices, you have to interpret the sections of dialogue where you think the character would be having these feelings while delivering the dialogue. Mark your sub-beats accordingly. All the feelings on the list are the common preliminary responses to realizing your truth is in fact false, an illusion. These feelings might be explained this way:

Anger. I'm pissed at myself for being so stupid and believing that illusion. I'm angry that my family and friends never set me straight.

Sadness. I'll miss my best friend, the illusion. I'm mourning the death of my best friend or the death of my identity.

Guilt. It's my fault I believed that illusion.

Embarrassment. How ridiculous, stupid, and silly I am for believing that illusion. **Note:** When playing an embarrassed sub-beat, keep it very light with giggles and moments of hiding, for example, holding your hand in front of your face or turning your face away. Writers will sometimes include an embarrassed sub-beat during a loss of illusion beat for variety's sake and to provide a brief respite from the heaviness of the other sub-beats. When playing embarrassment, don't confuse it with shame, which is very heavy.

Confused. If your character knows she's going through the loss of illusion: How did this ever happen? When did I buy into the illusion? Am I that dense? What do I do now?

If your character doesn't yet know he's going through the loss of illusion (because the body knows before the brain does and, despite real and authentic feelings, our brains don't always provide an accurate and truthful rendering of the situation.): I'm confused about what I'm going through. I don't know what it is. Why am I feeling all these emotions?

Snobbery. An overreaction intended to maintain and show some dignity that covers up what your body is really going through. The loss of the illusion makes your body feel like it's less than others, so you armor it to compensate, and that allows you to feel better, or superior to others. You know, or think you know, that dignity always prevails, that it's dignity that gives you the best chance of surviving what you are going through.

Defensive. It's not my fault that I lived by that illusion! Why didn't someone shake me and tell me it's not true?

Fear. I'm scared of what else may not be true. I'm scared of what happens now. I'm scared because of how blind I've been.

Bitterness. I'm bitter toward myself for being so stupid and for now having to accept this difficult truth. I'm bitter toward others or the world—it's their fault I bought the lie.

Disbelief. I can't believe how stupid I am for believing that illusion.

Shame. I really let myself down by believing that illusion. I'm smarter than that.

Frustration. I keep trying to make the illusion real, and it keeps slipping away (cf., Sisyphus' punishment).

Regret. I feel sorrow or repentance or distress over the loss of my best friend, the illusion.

Grief. I'm heartbroken and devastated over the death of my best friend, the illusion, or the death of my identity.

Despair. What now? How can I go on? The great abyss.

Most monologues with a crying stage direction contain about five to seven sub-beats, regardless of the length of the monologue. There is the occasional exception with four sub-beats or as many as nine. When you are in character and playing these choices, everything comes together and leads you to crying in the sadness or despair beats.

Following are two sample breakdowns. My breakdown choices are in **bold** and also indicate the sub-beat changes:

THREE SISTERS by A. Chekhov

In the third act, the brother, Andrei, speaking to his sisters, gives up the double illusions that he is happily married and successful.

Umbrella Arc: Loss of Illusion—He is happily married and successful

(Angry)

ANDREI: I just want to say this and then I'll go. Now... in the first place you have something against Natasha; I've seen it since the day we were married. I happen to think Natasha is a good, honest person; she's straightforward and honorable. I would like you to understand that I love and respect my wife; I respect her and I demand that respect from others. She is an honest, honorable person, and whatever you imagine are your grievances, I'm sorry, are just pure fabrications on your part. (Pause)

(Snob)

Secondly, you are apparently angry that I didn't finish my doctorate and that I'm not in research by now. I happen to serve on the City Council, and I think my work there is just as sacred and noble a calling as science. I'm a member of the City Council, I work hard and I have pride in my work there. (Pause)

(Guilty)

Third, there's something else it's necessary for me to say . . . It is true that I mortgaged the house without your consent . . . that was wrong, I know, and I ask you to forgive me . . . That action was necessitated by my debts . . . thirty-five thousand rubles . . . I don't play cards anymore; I gave all that up long ago; my only justification is that you girls, you received an allotment and I didn't . . . I have (Pause) nothing you could call income at all.

(Defensive)

They're not listening. Natasha is a fine, honest person. (Walks silently up and down, then stops.)

(Arc Sad→Despair)

When I was married I thought we'd be happy . . . but, my God . . . (Cries.) Oh, my dearest, darling sisters, it's not true. Don't believe me. Don't believe me . . . (He exits.)

KRAMER VS. KRAMER by Robert Benton

This monologue is from an early version of the screenplay and didn't make it into the final film. It's near the end of the script. After winning a custody trial, the mother (Meryl Streep) changes her mind and relinquishes custody of her son to her ex-husband (Dustin Hoffman) and gives up the illusion that she is a good mother.

Umbrella Arc: Loss of Illusion—She is a good mother

(Confused)

JOANNA

(a deep breath, then:)

Ted, when we got married it was because I was twenty-seven years old and I thought I should get married and . . . when I had Billy it was because I thought I should have a baby . . . and I guess all I did was mess up my life and your life and--

                    TED

          Joanna, what the hell is—

(Embarrassed)

                  JOANNA

                 (urgent)

          Please . . . Please don't stop me. This is the
          hardest thing I've ever had to do . . .

                  ON TED—struck by the urgency in her voice.

(Sad)

                  JOANNA

          After I left . . . when I was in California, I
          began to think, what kind of mother was
          I that I could walk out on my own child. It
          got to where I couldn't tell anybody about
          Billy—I couldn't stand that look in their
          faces when I said he wasn't living with me.

(Grief)

          Finally it seemed like the most important
          thing in the world to come back here and
          prove to Billy and to me and to the world
          how much I loved him . . . And I did . . . And I
          won. Only . . . it was just another "should."

(Despair)

                 (she begins to break down)
          . . . Sitting in that courtroom. Hearing
          everything you did, everything you went
          through . . . Something happened. I guess it
          doesn't matter how much I love him, or how

much you love him. I guess it's like you said, the only thing that counts is what's best for Billy. I don't know, maybe that's all love is anyway . . .

Ted, I think Billy should stay with you . . .

TED

(stunned)

What?

JOANNA

(she reaches out, takes his hand)
He's already got one mother, he doesn't need two . . . He's yours . . .

(her last ounce of reserve crumbles)
I won't fight you for him any more. He's yours...

TED

Oh, God . . . Oh, my God . . .

JOANNA

Only can I still see him?

TED

No more waiting in Coffee Shops . . . I promise.

Joanna's last ounce of reserve crumbles, she begins to sob. Ted puts his arms around her and holds her. They do not kiss.

How to Rehearse

The rehearsal approach is almost the same as for any monologue and can be found in Monologues: Breakdown and Rehearsal, How to Rehearse [p. 73]. Follow that procedure until you get to rehearsing the final sub-beat, sadness or despair, where the crying is meant to occur, and return here for the final steps of rehearsing.

Rehearsing the Final Sub-Beat

You have done the whole monologue except for the last sub-beat, labeled sadness or despair. This is the sub-beat with the stage directions for crying or the director's note to cry. This beat will probably be the final sub-beat of the whole monologue, but not always.

As you approach rehearsing the final sub-beat, get in touch with what your body is going through—it's going through a loss of illusion, the loss of your character's best friend. Her best friend was [*Name the character's illusion, for example, coming to Hollywood would bring her success; she would reconcile and have a loving relationship with her father; she would meet Mr. Right and get married and have children.*]When someone goes through a loss of illusion, sadness is the penultimate level of feeling, which then heightens to despair. Despair is the saddest of sadnesses; it's the top of the sad arc, sadder than everything else, including grief. When you're just sad, you kind of know in the back of your head that you're sad now, but it'll get better tomorrow. There's a light at the end of the tunnel. Life will be okay again. But when you're in despair, you feel like there's no light at the end of the tunnel. You feel like there is no tomorrow--that your life is over. It's just hopeless. There's no chance to get out of this horrible feeling of devastation, the death of your best friend—the illusion that you've been believing in all these years. Despair is where the crying is going to occur. It is not important that you cry at the exact placement of the stage direction for crying, only somewhere near it.

After you have done the whole loss of illusion beat or monologue except for the last sub-beat, run the whole monologue again, adding the last sadness or despair sub-beat. When you get to that sub-beat, physicalize sadness and stay open to doing an emotion arc, intensifying the feeling while saying the lines, and keep arcing sadness until it reaches its peak, despair and crying. The final sadness/despair sub-beat does not get its own rehearsal like the other preceding beats. It's done for the first time in a run-through of the whole loss of illusion beat or monologue. For more on intensifying feelings and doing an emotion arc see Emotion Arc [p. 51].

When you do this run-through, if you nail the sub-beats by fully physicalizing the sub-beat choices, something unique is going to happen (or it may have already happened in an earlier run-through). Somewhere during this run-through you will feel a tiny feeling of really deep, authentic sadness. It will be as noticeable to you as a pinprick. I call it a "seed." That part of your brain that remains the actor and not the character will spot the little seed and know the seed is where crying comes from. That's how vivid this little pinprick of sadness is. It will not feel like acting; it feels like you are about to enter a deep well of sadness, significantly deeper than any sadness you may have felt before with this material. We can't anticipate when you'll feel and notice the seed, but you will, so long as you don't mess up the previously rehearsed sub-beats.

In the first full run-through, when you feel that seed of authentic sadness, you have to water that seed until it grows into a big blossoming tree of crying. The growth of the seed is your acting challenge—with its appearance, the seed chose you, and you have to choose it back by growing it.

How to Water the Seed: You water the seed by heightening the physicalization of the feeling that comes from the seed, extending it through the whole body until you start crying. Whatever you feel your body doing, allow your body to do more of it. For example, perhaps you notice your body is relaxed without tension. Let it relax more, even to the point of almost collapsing. If the corners of your mouth are turning downward, turn them down more. If your exhales seem longer than your inhales, make them even longer. If your eyes feel less than fully open, close them a little more. Try squinting (without adding tension!). At the next sigh, add more sound and turn it into a whimper. Take a whimper further by extending the sound, perhaps into a sob. You are physically exploring and experimenting to find what it takes to let that seed grow and blossom into deep and authentic sad feelings and crying. It's different for each person. Nail the sub-beats and the seed will appear. You can then water it by heightening the physicalization. Keep heightening it until you are crying and then go with it. When you choose to stop crying, planned or in the moment, coming down will be authentic and works well with any remaining lines in the loss of illusion beat.

If the seed appears in another sub-beat before the sad/despair beat, and it's not a guilt sub-beat, leave it alone. Don't water it; it's not going anywhere. Keep physicalizing the remaining sub-beats the same way. When you get into the sadness, grief, or despair sub-beat, you'll see the seed will start to emerge again, and you will start your watering. In the unlikely event the seed doesn't come back, return to where you first felt it in your body. It's there, buried under the previous sub-beats. If the seed appears in a guilt sub-beat, water it, grow it, and go with it. Let your crying start there. If the seed doesn't show up until the end of the despair sub-beat, you have to water it (heighten the physicalization) a lot and fast.

If you nail your sub-beats, the sadness seed will appear magically because you're going through all the emotions that a person goes through when experiencing a loss of illusion. "Oh my God, something's happened. This is awful, I feel like my best friend has died." The seed appears because the brain, thanks to its capacity to learn through repetition and patterns, has formed a connection between loss and these emotions. But once the seed comes, it's on you to take charge of it, water it, and keep growing it to crying. In multiple run-throughs (or takes), the seed may appear at different points. If no seed appears, that tells you there is something wrong with your sub-beats. Either they are mislabeled or you are not nailing them with full and consistent physicalizations. If you think you may have mislabeled them, check to see if you have primarily used the choices from the list with asterisks (*). If not, reconsider your choices. Even though you did not have to remember all the sub-beat choices when you started this process, your body has now learned them because of the experiential work on each sub-beat and each run-through.

Physicalizing loss of illusion puts your body through the physiological components of a loss of illusion. Combined with your character's involvement in the story and saying the lines in the loss of illusion beat, physicalization takes you to the real experience. Your body will experience the feeling of devastation that always accompanies a loss of illusion and that enables the seed to appear, followed by the crying. Sometimes the character doesn't know or understand that he/she is going through a loss of illusion, but the body does. If that's the case, by the end of the monologue, the brain understands that you are letting go of the character's specific illusion.

Physicalizing the sub-beats and being in the moment also prevents you from being caught up in worrying about whether or not you are going to cry. Focusing and being committed to nailing each of the sub-beats and understanding how the choices make sense keeps you too busy.

Sometimes there is an extra and final sub-beat or *tag* that serves as an anticlimactic sub-beat after the crying. It is usually a very short sub-beat of one sentence, and the emotion choice is usually "embarrassed" (about having cried).

When you rehearse or perform, as you have success, make sure you *pour confidence back into the work.* Celebrate yourself and bring it into the work: "Oh look, I got the seed. This is great. That felt terrific. Let's do it again!" Then, as you water it, keep exploring new ways to water it; *experiment* with the physicalization of the different parts of your body. **Rehearsal tip:** After you have success with a few run-throughs, if you have a run-through where it's not happening, the moment you notice it's not happening, continue as if it is and see what you discover. Continue as if an audience is watching the run-through and try to fool the audience. Don't let them know that it's not working. Have your body act as if it is feeling the emotion. Think of it as if it's a film and you've got to finish the last shot of the day before losing the light. You can't say, "Sorry Meryl, I'm not feeling it. We'll have to do it again tomorrow." Or think of it as a theater performance and you can't quit in the middle. The paradox is that, if you're not feeling it, the more you act as if you are, the more you will actually feel it. **Warning:** If you don't know your lines cold, this solution won't work. Trying to remember lines interferes with the necessary physiological interplay between the body and the mind. **Suggestion:** Practice this process with one of the samples where the breakdown choices have been made for you.

★ Solution #2 — Physicalization and Breath

Physicalizing sadness will be easy and understandable if you practice the exercises for learning how to Physicalize an Emotion [p. 31]. Sadness requires relaxing your body with a slight sense of collapsing, tilting your head downwards slightly, partially opening your mouth with the corners turned down, glancing downward in an unfocused manner, and raising the inner ends of your eyebrows (like you are pulling them up and pushing them together in the center of the forehead). Wrinkles should form on your forehead. In short, have a sad face and body. Your brain will recognize what the body does when it is feeling sad and release the feeling. If you have learned and practiced physicalizing an emotion, the body's expression of sadness comes easily and spontaneously, without thinking of the individual body parts and what they do. Complete the physicalization by breathing from the diaphragm with a series of two to five quick and short inhalations through the nose, followed by a long exhalation through the mouth, until there is no breath left inside you. Begin the staccato inhalations through the nose again and repeat the process a few times. Physicalizing the breath, known as Alba Emoting, can be tricky to learn without a guide and practice. If you find that you can do the breath pattern, it will accelerate the process and heighten the intensity of the feeling, leading to crying sooner. If you use the breath pattern, when the scene is over make sure to lose the emotion by doing a Step-Out [p. 75].

On the other hand, physicalizing with the face and body without adding the breath pattern is sufficient to generate, heighten, and communicate sadness. Heightening the physicalization [see Solution #1: How to Water the Seed, p. 165] and going with it has a good chance of taking you to crying.

★ Solution #3 — Sad Arc

Designate the beginning and ending of the beat where the character cries. The beat should start where the character first feels sadness. The beat ends right after the crying occurs. When the beat starts, *physicalize* sadness. As the beat continues, heighten the physicalization at a pace that matches the length of the beat so that you arrive at crying where and when you want to [see Emotion Arc, p. 51]. Not only will you cry, but you will also make the whole beat culminating in the crying more dynamic, as the audience gets caught up in your sadness intensifying.

Arcing the sadness requires heightening the physicalization throughout the beat. Whatever your body is doing, do more of it. For examples of heightening a sadness physicalization, see Solution #1, How to Water the Seed [p. 165]. Find out what it takes for you to heighten the physicalization to crying. Learning and practicing a sad arc is approached in the same way as any emotion arc and can be found at Emotion Arc [p. 51]. Heightening the physicalization does not mean pushing, which will add tension and frustration and accomplish nothing. As in the previous solution, adding the breath pattern, if you can do it, at the top of the arc where you want to cry will increase your chances of success.

Solution #4 — As-If / Loss of Illusion

After designating the specific loss of illusion for the character, imagine a personal experience you can use in an as-if approach.

Think of something in your life you assume to be true that, if you discovered it was not, would leave you devastated. For example, a loved one you consider a good person is justly arrested or convicted for some heinous crime (your belief in this person's goodness was an illusion). How would that feel? Other examples: you or your parents divorce (your belief that you or your parents are happily married was an illusion); your partner cheats on you (your belief that your partner loves and respects you was an illusion); you will get around to losing 30 or more pounds when you are really ready to do so (your belief that a fit and healthy life is just around the corner was an illusion); you are forced to give up acting as a career choice (your belief that you can make it as a professional actor was an illusion). Your choice of an issue and the illusion must involve very high personal stakes.

Select your issue and illusion and play the scene as-if you are going through the loss of that illusion. It may be sufficient to empathize with the character and their loss of illusion now that you have compared it to something in your own life the truth of which is very important to you.

While rehearsing or preparing for "Action" to be called, relax your body and imagine the event that could initiate your loss of illusion. For example, your wife tells you she wants a divorce; a loved one is arrested or convicted; you don't have an acting gig lined up and will soon have to default on your mortgage; you eat a quart of ice cream in one sitting.

Then, in your mind's eye, see the details of your chosen situation in the same fashion as an affective or emotional memory [Play a Specific Emotion, Solution #3, p. 133], replacing the memory with the imagined situation and, in addition, seeing the person (or object) who is responsible for your loss of the illusion. Receive the communication that triggers your giving up your illusion.

By now, the feeling of sadness should be emerging in your body. Other feelings may appear first; examples include confusion, anger, and guilt. If so, allow your body to go with it and avoid any resistance to these feelings, but don't dwell very long with them. These emotional changes during a shot on you will not be cut, and the final change will always be to sadness. When you start feeling sad, you will feel your body relaxing—go with it. Let the feeling grow. *Stay aware of how your body is responding to the process.* Examples of physical responses to feeling sad are found in Solution #2 [p. 168]. To the best of your ability, observe the details of what's going on with your body while maintaining this rising feeling of sadness. Should the observation of these details impede the power of the imagined situation, stay with the situation and let go of the observation. Or not.

While you are feeling the sadness, perhaps you've begun to cry. Run the part of the scene where the script or director wants you to cry, staying focused on your loss-of-illusion situation *as much as you need to* in order to fuel how you feel (sad and crying). As with the Affective Memory, it's best to run it a few times to discover and take advantage of any *triggers* [see Play a Specific Emotion, Solution #3, p. 133, for a discussion of locating a trigger for the emotion, substituting imagination for memory and sad for angry].

If you have not found a trigger, a shortcut will enable quicker access to the feeling and serve you well when you need the feeling on multiple takes or setups or if the feeling is fading during a take or performance. Instead of re-creating the situation, just *physicalize* those body details you were noticing earlier in the process. Your brain will recognize what the body does when it is feeling sad and crying, and it will release that feeling. When physicalizing, you don't have to be concerned about "indicating" or performing some generalized or cliché form of the emotion if you *physicalize all parts of your body* while listening, saying your lines, and doing any business.

There are many different variations of *as-if*. It can sometimes be as easy as picking a situation that will provoke the crying, for example, "It's as if my boyfriend died." Ideally, the less you focus on the imagined situation while playing the scene, the better. You can let the imagined situation activate your feelings as a preparation for the scene.

Solution #5 — Subtext/Secret

The subtext is what the character is focused on while talking about something else. The scene's power comes from not talking about the subtext even as it influences what you are thinking and saying. It also influences behavior, business, and relationships.

To bring about crying, give yourself a sad secret, unknown to the other characters or the audience. It can be your character's secret or your own. A character's secret is better because it's more grounded as a part of your whole performance and may lead you to interesting discoveries about your character or the script. A personal secret can suffice if you find it to be rich and stimulating. Regardless of whether you go personal or character, no one will ever know your secret except you. If you have designated the crying as a result of a loss of illusion, perhaps your secret is related to the illusion or its loss. Here are some examples of sad secrets: a loved one is dying or has just died; you have just been diagnosed with a terminal illness; you or a loved one are going to prison for a long time; your partner has just dumped you; you are not really talking to the other characters but to the spirit of a dead loved one. While preparing for "Action," focus on your secret.

At "Action," focusing on the secret becomes the subtext you are fully focused on as you play the here and now of the scene, going with the feelings arising from the secret until you start crying. How long you stay focused on the secret will depend on the extent and intensity of crying required. Ideally, the less you focus on the secret while playing the scene, the better. It's best if you can let the secret activate your feelings as a preparation for the scene and, when it's time to cry, use as needed. Whenever you are focusing on the secret, allow your body to respond to it. Don't dictate your body's physicalized response.

Solution #6 — Affective or Emotional Memory

If you can identify a real-life situation from your past in which you experienced deep sadness and crying, you can use that memory as a springboard into feeling it now [see Play a Specific Emotion, Solution #3—Affective or Emotional Memory, p. 133]. Instead of the anger experience referenced there, use your choice of a sad experience. When you get to examples of physical details you observe resulting from the process, you can substitute examples of feeling sad as found in Solution #2—Physicalization and Breath [p. 168]. Your brain will recognize what your body does when it is feeling sad and crying and release that feeling. Don't forget to play the scene with the emotion, instead of dwelling on the emotion alone. In other words, don't let your acting become self-indulgent. Illuminate the character, not your exploitation of acting effects.

Solution #7 — Makeup

There are tools supplied by the makeup person to assist in crying and creating tears:

Eyedrops. The makeup person will apply a drop to the inner corner of your eye as you tilt your head slightly back. As "Action" is called, you will straighten your head and a tear will roll down.

Petroleum jelly–based product. The makeup person will apply the product, Vaseline or Aquaphor, with a cotton swab under and on the side of the eye to make you look like you have been crying. The product can also stimulate further crying.

Tear stick. The makeup person will apply this menthol-based product like a lipstick under the eyes. Like petroleum jelly, this product can make you look as if you have been crying and also stimulate further crying.

Menthol air blow. The makeup person will use a little gizmo to blow menthol air into your eye that will irritate it, make it turn red, and produce tears.

Other makeup aids. The makeup person can apply illuminator under the foundation to reflect light and help tears glow; use waterproof cosmetics and setting spray to keep everything intact.

When using these makeup solutions, don't forget to have a sad face and body. Understand that using these solutions will also mean that you may not have provided the director with a single take in which you go from no tears to tears on camera. The director will have to cut away from you before the tears so the makeup person can apply the aid and then cut back to you. Watch a crying scene and rewind to when you last saw the character without tears. The director cuts away to someone else and then back to the character for the emergence of the tears, possibly to cover up the introduction of a makeup tool. After any application of makeup, don't touch your face. When I was a young apprentice in summer stock, I was cast in a small part in a star package summer stock tour of *Never Too Late*, with Dennis O'Keefe and Betty Field. I played a cop who came to their house to tell them to keep the noise down. Prior to my entrance on opening night, I waited backstage and rubbed my eyes out of nervousness, forgetting I was wearing mascara. When Dennis answered the door and I entered, he gave me his first lines and then ad-libbed another: "And who gave you those black eyes?" I learned to look in a mirror before entering.

Solution #8 — Don't Cry — Fight to Hold Back Tears

There's a well-known saying in acting classes: "If you cry, the audience doesn't have to. But if you don't cry, the audience will cry for you." David Mamet expresses the same basic idea: "Tears are like homeopathic medicine: the smaller the dose, the greater effect." Using any of the preceding solutions or any approach to crying, add an additional step: as you feel yourself about to cry, don't. Hold it back. You don't want the other characters to see you cry. Your approach now includes resisting the tears. Offer the director an additional take in which you hold the crying back.

While the above paragraph has merit, you should cry when the stage directions call for it or the director has requested it. Not crying is a viable and powerful option for those occasions when crying surprises you, the stage directions and the director having never mentioned it. Through the spontaneity and conviction of your performance, you feel that you are about to cry. Do everything you can to not cry. Let the camera and audience see that struggle. The struggle is dynamic to watch. It is what many people experience when they feel the urge to cry. It is vulnerable and honest.

All Solutions

Music

"Music is the shorthand of emotions," Tolstoy said. Some actors find that listening to particular music selections induces feelings of sadness and helps them get into the mood for crying.

Tears / No Tears

There are occasions when the actor is crying without actual tears emerging. As Gregory David Roberts writes, "Sometimes we love with nothing more than hope. Sometimes we cry with everything except tears." While everyone is born capable of shedding real tears, our individual life stories may hinder this ability. We might learn in adolescence to cover up feelings instead of experiencing and processing them. Viola Spolin points out that "as we grow older, we muscularly *hold* many manifestations of feeling. As a result of cultural pattern, we are forced to *hold* our tears and stifle our laughter." When Sally Field was asked by a student about the student's difficulty reaching real tears, Sally replied, "You may not be ready for that." In this situation, practice opening the door to the emotional self. Being available to access one's authenticity, vulnerability, and empathy might be the necessary requirement for real tears. You might practice by crying without any suppression of your feelings as an audience member in the darkness of a movie theater, or the privacy of your home, when the characters on screen move you to do so. Engage in their feelings. Allow yourself to be moved. You want to become comfortable with crying, the awareness and feeling of your own tears, seeing your red eyes in the mirror right after you cry.

You may not be hydrated enough to cry. Try drinking a liter of water an hour before needing to cry. If you want water to come out of you, it may be a good idea to have water inside of you.

Tears are not as important as feeling like you are crying and your face and body showing this feeling—in other words, physicalization. In many crying scenes in films, theater, and TV, the actor is crying and there are no tears. The character's vulnerability and sadness are so authentic and vivid the audience is deeply moved, and unless they're paying very close attention, never notices there are no actual tears. *Boogie Nights* features a great example of an actor crying without tears. Julianne Moore's character, a porn actor and drug addict, has just lost a custody battle for her child. The scene cuts to her leaning against a wall outside and sobbing and sobbing and sobbing. No tears . . . and an Academy Award nomination for Best Supporting Actress. In another scene in the same film, Philip Seymour Hoffman also cries without tears as he sits in a car after making a failed pass at his friend (played by Mark Wahlberg).

Finally, in order to reach tears when you are crying in sadness, make sure there is no tension in your body when you need to cry. Crying while angry or frightened can be effective, but you are not likely to reach tears unless you, first, take a quick moment to release the body's tensions and allow your body to relax as you commence the crying. I believe that not doing this is why Philip Seymour Hoffman was tearless in his crying scene. He cries while feeling and displaying anger at himself for making a pass at his friend. His angry body is full of tension and he never dissipates it.

Loss of Illusion — Happy Ending

While loss of illusion is common enough in real life, it is highlighted in scripts due to its dramatic potential. Characters go through a loss of illusion because it serves the script's theme and the character's arc. For instance, the character goes from inauthenticity to authenticity. Crying is very dramatic and compelling to watch. In scripts, as in real life, the loss of illusion creates a period of deep unhappiness that might be brief or might go on for a very long time, even years. People heal on their own schedules. Regardless of how much time it takes, the unhappiness caused by loss of illusion will often gradually diminish until it's gone. Living, for the first time, an authentic life, free of illusion, the character is happier. In scripts, this period of happily moving on with your life usually occurs in the anticlimactic final scene of a film or in the unwritten scenes that would follow the final curtain. You might see a hint of the good news to come, but the writer doesn't need to go into that. It is a testament to the writer's ability that we understand anyway that the character is going to be all right. Sometimes the writer spells it out, as, for example, in the title character's final affirmation in *Dear Evan Hansen*: "Dear Evan Hansen, Today is going to be a good day and here's why. Because today, no matter what else, today at least . . . you're you. No hiding, no lying. Just . . . you. And that's . . . that's enough." As we read in the Bible (John 8:32), "Ye shall know the truth, and the truth shall make you free."

WHEN YOU NEED TO

LAUGH

Laughing on cue, repeatedly and authentically and at something that may not even be funny, can be one of the most challenging skills an actor needs.

★ Solution #1 — Peanut Butter

Just before entering on stage for your laughing scene or going to the set for your laughing shot, fill your belly button with peanut butter. When you need to laugh, think about the peanut butter and where it is.

★ Solution #2 — Physicalize Emotion + Breath

This solution is outstanding for its authenticity, repeatability, and ease of control for intensity—everything from small giggles to rolling on the floor uncontrollably. Physicalizing happy is easy and may be accomplished by smiling and keeping your face and body relaxed and loose, with no tension anywhere in the body. The breath pattern may be tricky to learn without practice. As you try it, make sure you keep your face and body relaxed and a smile on your face, the bigger the better. Breathe with a light and quick inhale through the nose, followed by an exhale through the mouth that has multiple quick staccatos (*ha-ha-ha-ha-ha-ha*) for as long as it takes to get all the air out before the next inhale. Don't add tension near the end of the exhale when you are getting the last of the breath out. Instead, heighten the relaxation and make the smile bigger. You have to go with it and enjoy making the smile bigger as you bottom out the exhale and a joyous feeling takes you over. Build the charge with your staccatos, which will turn into involuntary muscle movements in the lower abdomen. It is these muscle movements that will coincide with your laughs. When the laughs begin to subside, inhale and start the process again. Build the charge.

After you have practiced with the breath pattern and are confident in your ability to employ it, you can control the intensity of the laughing by adjusting the size of your smile. The bigger the smile, the bigger the laughs.

When you try the breath pattern for the first time, you may be so focused on getting it right that you will forget about the physicalization and it won't work. Try it again and first physicalize a happy body—relaxed and, most importantly, with a happy face! Smile, the bigger the better, so big that your eyes feel involved. It's not likely you will have really happy eyes without a smile. Use Horizontal (diaphragm or belly) Breathing [see Deal with Being Nervous, Solution #4, p. 187]. Vertical breathing (in which your shoulders and upper chest move up and down) adds tension to the body. For real joy, inhale and exhale from the diaphragm (belly). Don't inhale through the nose like a vacuum cleaner with deep, powerful suction. Keep it light and quick through the nose, pulling the air in from the diaphragm. As the pattern kicks in, the staccatos are the laughs. Continue the staccatos while you exhale all the breath prior to the next inhale. Even when you think all the breath is out, it's not. Go further with one or more staccatos, without adding tension. Then do the next inhale. Putting too much desire, attention, and energy into doing it absolutely correctly is a common problem. You are replacing your relaxation with stress. Stress or tension anywhere in the body and not having a smile on your face will prevent the pattern from working. Some actors think they are smiling when they are not. To make any smile requires upturned lip corners. If you find yourself getting into your head, notice it, let it go, smile, and start the pattern. If you are having difficulty learning the pattern, try it lying down on your side in the fetal position. Keep your eyes open. When you have success a few times, return to standing or sitting.

After you have practiced the pattern, all it takes to laugh on cue is the quick and light inhale and allowing your body to go into the physicalization and the pattern.

Solution #3 — Method Choices

See Play a Specific Emotion, Solutions #3, #4, and #5 [p. 133-140], and choose for your *affective* or *emotional memory*, *substitution*, or *as-if*, a happy and funny choice. Prepare ahead of time with a list of choices for multiple performances or takes. When one goes dry, switch the choice.

WHEN YOU NEED TO

LEAVE YOUR ACTED EMOTIONS BEHIND AND GO ON TO THE NEXT SCENE OR GO HOME

When you finish a scene and are about to move on to another scene, or when it's time to go home after a rehearsal, performance, or day of shooting, you may feel the need to get rid of any lingering emotional residue.

★ Solution

Do the following **Step-Out**:

Pick a spot at eye level on a wall across the room. Look at that one spot and take five slow, long breaths, inhaling through the nose for five counts and exhaling through the mouth for five counts. Don't strain yourself. If you can't do five counts, do three or four. Continue for one minute. When you finish the breaths, do some full-body stretching and simultaneously speak gibberish out loud. Continue for one minute. With the fingertips of both hands, gently pat all over your face like you're playing the piano. Each finger tap should be a gentle expression of you loving yourself. Simultaneous with the finger taps, out loud in a very soothing voice, say affirmations to yourself—for example, "Hello, I love you. I love you. How is my old friend? Here we are together again. There are my lips. This is my nose. Here is my forehead. Hello." Continue for thirty seconds. Bend over and pat your knees with your open hands. Continue for 10 seconds. Like magic, your emotional residue will have disappeared.

WHEN YOU NEED TO DEAL WITH BEING NERVOUS

Most actors experience nerves in one form or another. It goes with the gig and you're in good company. In order to deal with nervousness prior to performing (and without going into the multitude of reasons actors get nervous), I find this explanation by novelist Neil Gordon illuminating:

"Did you ever, when you were a child, stand on a cliff above a lake and will yourself to jump? You know there is no danger. That when you find the will to step into the air, your body will writhe to its balance, that the water will crash around your face in a brilliant flash of green, and that, laughing, you'll rise to the surface in a tunnel of bubbles exploding against the sun. Yet with all you know, with all you want to jump, before the act itself a paralysis overtakes you. It is not the height, it is not the cold of the water—these are there, but are not what stop you. It's the consciousness that before you is a decision, and, trivial or not, once taken, it cannot be revoked."

In the theater, it's waiting for your cue to enter or, as Elaine Stritch said, "The scariest word in the world is . . . Places!" In camera acting, it's waiting for "Action." An argument can be made that theater nerves are more crippling than camera nerves. After all, in camera acting, you can always muck up a take and they will call "Cut" and you'll have another chance. In the theater, once you enter, there's no going back. Katharine Cornell, "The First Lady of the Theater," a reigning Broadway star of the second quarter of the twentieth century, got so nervous she threw up before every performance. Theater lore has it that on opening night of *The Odd Couple* on Broadway, Walter Matthau grumbled to the stage manager before his first entrance, "If you think I'm going out there, you're f'ing crazy." Nevertheless, if you have ever shot a scene as a co- or guest star on a TV series with minimal rehearsal, you know how easily your nerves can work against you. It never really goes away, even for movie stars. Hugh Grant speaks of "absurd stage fright attacks" that would hit him in the middle of filming without warning. He adds, "Nerves are your massive enemy in film acting."

Being well prepared for your performance is the best foundation for reducing your anxieties and having a reasonable amount of nervous energy.

There are also positive aspects of nerves and fear because they can serve a purpose. They are there for you to face and overcome. For some, the adrenaline raised when nervous becomes the juice with which you start your performance and which can take you to levels deep inside that you didn't know were there. Meryl Streep supports this view: "Fear is a good thing. Fear is your friend. Everything that destabilizes you can help you. They taught us that in drama school. If you're comfortable, you're not doing your job. Most actors are constitutionally insecure. It's sort of necessary."

Before going on to the solutions, there is a preliminary approach that will serve you well regardless of the solution you choose. Dealing with the fear and finding the courage to do what you have to do begins with honesty. In the moment you experience these feelings of fear, be honest. Observe that you *are* experiencing and feeling them. Do not attempt to diminish the feelings through lying, rationalizing, explaining, or denying. Your body is the source of the feelings; it will know that you are lying. Lying to your body will exacerbate the very feelings you are trying to dissipate. Notice that you are nervous or frightened and acknowledge it—"I'm nervous. I'm scared. I'm frightened." Honestly naming the feelings or emotions can calm your brain and reduce stress. You become the feeling's partner, rather than its victim, and that's a much more powerful position. Naming the feeling or emotion without explaining, diminishing, or embellishing it reads much easier than doing it. A simple exercise in naming emotions will serve you well if you practice it. The exercise is found in Physicalizing an Emotion, Optional [p. 49].

Here are a few solutions for alleviating your nerves prior to performing.

★ Solution #1 — Get Present

Do the 40 breaths process. Sit up straight with your feet flat on the floor. Take 10 big breaths—not slowly, but not rushed—with your eyes open. Inhale and exhale through the mouth. Put emphasis on the inhale, which should take a half of a second, directed to the center of your chest, then relax your exhale, about 2 seconds. Immediately start your next inhale. Take 10 of these breaths. Pause for three seconds and repeat the 10 breaths. Repeat the process two more times. You have now done *40 breaths*. Look around the room and name, out loud, objects and their colors ("The floor is gray. There is a silver lamp. That is a green wall.") Do about five of these object/color sentences (whole sentences and not just a list of colors). Now you are relaxed, present, and ready for the take or entrance. If you feel dizzy during or after the 40 breaths (which is rare), press into your feet, flat on the floor, and proceed to the object/color statements. The dizziness will disappear by the time you finish the statements. If you feel tingling in your limbs, that's good. It means the breathing worked and you have successfully oxygenated your blood. You can do the 40-breaths process standing if you prefer. I'm told that Denzel Washington uses a similar process before every take.

★ Solution #2 — Get In Your Body

Stand up straight with your feet flat on the floor and your arms at your side, or lie down on your back with your legs straight out and your arms at your side. Raise one arm up over your head to its full extension with your eyes on your rising hand all the way up, and lower it back to your side. Do the same thing with your other arm. Raise and lower each arm 10 times. Keep your eyes on the rising and falling hand.

Repeat the above with one addition: As you raise and lower one arm, simultaneously raise and lower the opposite knee to waist height. Let the leg bend at the knee, creating a 90-degree angle. Keep your eyes on the rising and falling hand. Lowering the foot to the floor, stamp it down with impact. Raise and lower each arm and leg about 10 times. You can stop when the sets become quick and automatic. If you are doing this sequence standing, you are finished.

If you're lying down, after the above sequence, instead of raising and lowering your arm straight up and down, raise your arm and touch the floor just above the opposite shoulder. Simultaneously, raise the opposite knee and cross your leg over the other leg, lowering the knee and foot on the outside of the opposite leg until the foot presses to the floor with impact. Return your arm and leg to their original positions. Do the same with the other arm and the other leg. Keep your eyes on the rising and falling hand. Raise and lower each arm and leg about 10 times. You can stop when the sets become quick and automatic. This sequence is called the *cross crawl*. When you are finished, you will feel centered and grounded.

★ Solution #3 — Do a Step-Out

Do the Step-Out process from Leave your Acted Emotions Behind and Go On to the Next Scene or Go Home [p. 182].

★ Solution #4 — Horizontal (diaphragm) Breathing

Changing your breathing from vertical to horizontal is another successful relaxation technique. If your shoulders rise and fall and your chest pushes out when you breathe, you are a vertical breather and not using your diaphragm. A horizontal breather inhales to the diaphragm, pushing the belly out. When you breathe, put your hand on your stomach just above your navel. If it pushes out as you inhale and deflates as you exhale, and there is also no up and down movement from your shoulders, you are breathing horizontally. Practice horizontal breathing, inhaling through the nose and exhaling through the mouth. When it feels natural, add a count to it. At first, do a two-count inhale and two-count exhale. When that's easy, extend the count to three in and three out, then four. Finally, go to a five. If you want to keep going, reverse the process: 5-4-3-2. If you experience difficulty, lie on your back, knees bent, and breathe in slowly and deeply through your nose as your belly rises but your chest remains still. Then tighten your abdominal muscles and exhale through pursed lips. Science tells us that vertical or shoulder breathing uses auxiliary muscles and produces a higher heart rate, blood pressure, and cortisol (stress hormone). Horizontal or diaphragmatic breathing is more conducive to calmness. It's an ancient technique that quiets the body and mind by engaging the parasympathetic nervous system.

Solution #5 — Security Charm

Carry with you, in your costume, a small personal and comforting possession—for example, a rabbit's foot, a good luck charm, a piece of Linus' blanket. Knowing it's there and, if necessary, touching it can ground you and ease anxiety.

Solution #6 — Magic Time

What you say to yourself waiting for your entrance or "Action" may have a calming effect. Remind yourself that *you are as good as the best thing you have ever done.* According to Jack Lemmon, this is what Billy Wilder told him at the start of shooting the classic comedy *Some Like It Hot*, when Jack was nervous about performing most of the film masquerading as a woman. He received an Oscar nomination for Best Actor in a Leading Role. No matter the film or play, while waiting for "Action" or just prior to his entrance, Jack always said to his scene partners or the crew, "It's magic time!" Barbra Streisand took a 27-year break from performing because of stage fright: "I don't get nervous nervous, but I don't enjoy it. I get scared. I don't want to disappoint people." She addressed the fear and returned to live performances by telling herself right before performing, "Let go and let God." The Broadway star Dorothy Stickney had a lifelong battle with stage fright and learned one lesson: "When panic overtook me and I felt absolutely unable to go on, I would tell myself, 'You don't have to do the whole play—you don't even have to play the next scene—all you have to do is say the next line.'"

X

CHARACTER

Oscar- and Emmy-winning actor Olivia Colman deliciously described her work: "I am just an actor—all I do is I memorize someone else's words and tart around." This section deals with how to "tart" around and the adjustments that may be required.

Most actors have their own approach to creating a character. It might start with respecting the writer's character description in the script, what other characters say about the character, and what the character says about himself, including his likes and dislikes. It might include biography writing or using a character-building catalyst—for example, animals, imaginary or body (energy) centers, gestures, status, archetypes, voice, costumes, and makeup. What happens when actors find out that the character they have created isn't working? In the theater, this is not that big of a problem because there is rehearsal time for re-creating. On a film or TV set, realizing your character isn't working hits hard, as there is too little time to go back to the drawing board and create a whole new character from scratch. As Viola Davis said, "When we get to the set, it's about figuring out how to make the character work and having the tools to be able to do that."

It's the director's responsibility to interpret the script and have a vision for the entire production. He may tell you your character is evil, or a nerd, or a con man, or a bitch. Based on my experience, there's a good chance he will be right. He has been working on the whole script and he understands how the parts fit together. You have probably been working on only your part and may not have considered how your character harmonizes with the whole story. I was coaching an actor for a film, a teen rom-com, in which he played the high school boyfriend of the female lead. She goes off to college and meets and develops a friendship with another guy (the male lead and hero). As the film moves on, the original boyfriend (my client) becomes jealous and starts doing dastardly stuff to the male lead. During coaching, my client told me he had worked with the female lead on their scenes, and they decided it was important to show how sincere their love for each other is in the early part of the film. After we ran those scenes, I pointed out that his portraying this sincerity was turning the scenes flat and boring. He didn't realize that his part of the whole script was to be the black hat, the bad guy. When he starts doing the dastardly stuff to the hero, resulting in a major conflict between them at the climax of the film, he would have to become a whole new character, Mr. Evil, and no longer Mr. Sincerity. This was a teen rom-com, and a Pauly Shore one at that. He understood my point. We rebuilt his character so that his early scenes with her had a subtle edge to them. He now had a hidden agenda, a subtext—to get laid and to keep her from going away to college the next day. The point of my story is that, when preparing a part, you might not take into account the other parts of the script and how you fit into them. If the director feels the need to tell you his judgment of the character, it might be valuable information for you to hear and discuss.

[Reminder: Many of the solutions throughout the book involve the **Secret Magic Stuff** that I find to be most effective with the quickest results. Those solutions are highlighted by a star ★.]

WHEN YOU NEED TO

QUICKLY CHANGE TO THE DIRECTOR'S VISION OF THE CHARACTER

Directors will usually give you an opportunity to explore and demonstrate your character. If they think you are going in the wrong direction, they will ask for a change. They get frustrated when it seems you are not hearing them and nothing changes in the character portrayal. The problem is heightened when you are on a shooting set and the director expects you to come up with a new characterization in fairly quick order. Michelle Williams talks about facing that possibility: "So that first day that you show up, you just sort of cross your fingers and hope that your preparation has led you down the right path and that you're going to hold hands and walk through it together, but you just don't know."

★ Solution

A complete character transformation to the director's vision can be achieved in less than 15 minutes by using an Attitude Line. Any additional time for rehearsal provides opportunity for further in-depth exploration of the character. When off set with more time available, such as when you first prepare the role, or during rehearsals for a stage production, the attitude line is also recommended as an essential tool for developing a character.

For a full understanding of attitude lines and their usage, see Attitude Lines: Process and Archetype [p. 9]. Here, I will focus on taking advantage of the director's input when he requests a new character portrayal.

Picking an Attitude Line

As you listen to the director's comments (you may have to help her along with prodding or questions), pay special attention to descriptions of the character's personality. What you are looking for is the basic attitude that serves as the foundation of the character's personality. The director might not refer to it explicitly, and asking for it might not be fruitful. Early in shooting *The Graduate*, the director, Mike Nichols, wasn't pleased with Anne Bancroft's characterization of Mrs. Robinson. He felt she was too nice. He offered her a line reading for "Benjamin, will you drive me home?" She said, "Oh! I can do that. That's *anger.*" She then took on anger as her basic attitude and thereby made Mrs. Robinson a character for posterity and received an Oscar nomination for Best Actress. Sometimes the director will name the attitude without referring to it as an attitude. If the director says the character has a real zest for life, what attitude is implied? You might consider "enthusiastic." You would then need to get in touch with what these attitudes feel like and how your attitude choice can be at the core of the character the director wants to see.

When you have as much description as you are going to get, reduce it to a core attitude line. An attitude line is a personal expression of the attitude, worded as succinctly and directly as possible: I'm angry; I'm enthusiastic; I'm insecure; Nobody loves me; I'm sweet; I'm lonely; I'm mean; I'm the best; I love life; I'm pretty; I'm smart; I'm the smartest; I'm happy; I'll try anything; I'm impatient; I'm worth it; I know best [see Appendix D for a lengthy list of Sample Attitude Lines, p. 272]. Avoid being clever (for example, "I'm the meanest SOB in the valley"). Hit the nail on the head and articulate it in three words or less. In each attitude line, there should be only one idea expressed, so avoid 'because' (Any attitude line with the word "because" will automatically contain at least two ideas, a cause and effect). While the scriptwriter probably did not employ a specific attitude line in creating his characters, he certainly imagined, visualized, and created a specific and different personality for each character. The foundation of that personality is the character's attitude. Every character has a consistent basic attitude that can be expressed in an attitude line.

If you have difficulty figuring out the attitude line from the director's comments, you may profit from picking an archetypal attitude line that comes close to the director's description. If there is time for searching through the text, you will be able to select the character's unique attitude line from the clues in the text [for more information on selecting an attitude line, and for a list of archetypal attitude lines, see Attitude Lines: Process and Archetypes, p. 9].

Creating the complete character, inner and outer, requires taking on the attitude with the body. Jack Nicholson said that when he prepares a role, "What I have always done is not necessarily have to act but become the physicality of the person." The simple process can be done in less than 15 minutes and is detailed in Attitude Lines: Process and Archetypes [p. 9].

After completing the attitude line process, return to the set. The character the director didn't like is completely gone and has been replaced with a new character. You will be in the character's body and have his attitude and personality.

If you have time to go through the script and find clues to your attitude line choice that don't match with the director's vision, discuss it with the director. If she doesn't come around and still insists it's the way she sees it, choose an attitude line that will support her vision. She's the boss. And she may be right.

WHEN YOU NEED TO

MAKE THE CHARACTER MORE PHYSICALLY DISTINCTIVE

Even when it seems to you that you have captured the essence of the character, the director might give you a note to make the character bigger or more physically distinctive. Here is a solution that will help solve the problem and add some pizazz to your characterization.

★ Solution

Make sure you have included and embodied the character's essence or attitude in your characterization [see Attitude Lines: Process and Archetypes, p. 9].

Rehearse a scene and finish with a run-through of the scene, preferably with your cast mate or an understudy. A stand-in reading for the other character(s) will suffice so long as you are performing your part of the run-through fully in character. Using a smartphone or any video recording device, shoot the run-through, always keeping your character's full body in the frame.

Watch the video with the sound off (to avoid getting caught up in self-critique or judgment). Pay close attention to your physicality, especially your arms and hands, feet and legs, and facial expressions. You are noticing the gestures your body creates. I call them gestures, but they could also be distinctive postures, facial expressions, or sounds. Write a list of the gestures you see yourself making, just a quick description of each one. There is no need to mention when you did the gesture. Examples include: finger(s) tapping, thumbs twiddling, palms rubbing each other, snapping fingers, fist pumps, prayer hands, clasping hands with fingers intertwined, pointing, scratching, nose pinching, face touches, brushing or sweeping back or playing with your hair, arm sweeps, hand(s) to belly or any part of the body, one or both hands on hip or gesturing out, sitting posture, crossing legs while seated and twirling foot, rubbing hands on thighs, scrunching face, pouting, extending lower lip, licking lips, grinning and laughing, big open eyes, rubbing eyes, handling eyeglasses, putting a finger in your ear, pulling up your pants, unique walking gait, cigarette or any object handling (including picking up or lifting, placing, throwing, pulling, pushing, tearing or ripping).

Watch the video again with the sound on and add to your list any sounds you make—for example, grunts, hisses, snorts, and chuckles. Avoid getting caught up with critiquing or evaluating your acting. Just focus on completing your list.

Your list probably includes 3-10 gestures. Review your list for gestures that have potential for embellishing, enlarging, or expanding the character, choosing 3-6. Promising gestures include: those involving movement (for example, tracing the surface of your face with a finger); gestures you made more than once (likely very natural and familiar to you); unique gestures (unfamiliar enough to stand out to you, for example, touching your tongue with a finger). Still gestures may also be promising (your arm across your waist or your hand on your hip) if you consider their impact on your posture or how your body arrived at them.

Rehearse by yourself. Get into your character and, without dialogue, work on one gesture at a time from your final list. Depending on the gesture, you can work walking, standing, or seated. Do the gesture a few times until it's familiar. Using the gesture as a starting point, play with it and experiment and discover variations or alterations of the original gesture. For example, while doing the original gesture, heighten or enlarge it and see where that takes you. You can extend or expand the gesture so more of your body is involved and see what that leads to, or intensify it until it feels significantly stronger, or explore it until it changes in some fashion. Can you include other parts of the body to make it more distinctive or stronger? Notice if the body feels like it wants to go in a certain direction (forward, backward, sideways). Don't feel the gesture always has to be done in the same direction. Use the space, behind, above, below, and in front of you and see where that leads you. Perhaps a part of the gesture interests you and has potential for developing. What you are looking for is something you like, a variation of the gesture that appeals to you. Explore and play with the gesture until you discover a movement, posture, facial expression, or sound that you like. If one of your listed gestures is a sound, play with that. For example, you can heighten a chuckle into howls of laughter; intensify a sigh into weeping. Not every gesture will lead to a discovery, but many will. You will know when playing with the gesture is productive because you will like what you discover and how your body responds to it and adopts it. You can easily feel how it fits and fills out your character. Your response to a specific gesture might be "Oh, I like that. That's fun. That's an interesting way to hold and smoke the cigarette and it's perfect for the character." Don't rush the process. Sometimes the body will move very quickly into a new gesture if it intuitively feels right. Sometimes it takes more time to play and explore the gesture further. The new gesture should affect you and not just feel mechanical. Engage the whole body with the new gesture, especially the legs and feet. Avoid designing a variation in your head and then fulfilling it with your body. Instead, play with the gestures as I have suggested and let your body discover the variations. Let the body lead you. When you discover a new variation you like, practice it a few times until you create muscle memory and you make it your own—that is, it's effortless and full of self-awareness of what you are doing. Own it to the point of knowing exactly what you're doing so that, in the moment when you're performing, you don't have to think about it, you can let go, and your body will take over and complete the gesture. Go through this process for each of the gestures on your list. It's important to practice without dialogue because doing so prevents you from planning when you will do the gestures. Build a collection or repertoire of the new gestures you now own.

The repertoire is a collection of the new individual gestures and may include something as small as how you hold a cigarette or cup of tea or as large as how a single finger point becomes your whole arm sweeping up and pointing with five fingers. Don't be concerned with the order of gestures in your new repertoire or connecting one gesture to another. Refresh the character's attitude or essence and practice the gestures in your new repertoire in character until you do them easily and with confidence. Be open to discoveries about the style of your character portrayal. For example, you may discover he's elegantly expressive.

Return to rehearsing the scene with your rehearsal partner(s) and do a run-through of the scene. For this run-through, focus on introducing and integrating gestures from your new repertoire. *Whenever you have an impulse to gesture or feel an opportunity to gesture, do a gesture from your new repertoire, integrate it into your characterization, and go with it.* Trust that you will spontaneously know in the moment when to draw from your repertoire. You are not limited to gestures from the new repertoire. Original gestures, as well as brand-new gestures, may emerge as you discover and become a deeper and more fully integrated character during this run-through. You may also surprise yourself with brand-new gestures that your body notices on its own and develops further to enhance the character. In other words, if you discover new gestures, go with them. Your character becomes more physically distinctive as you provide some or all of the gestures, old and new, in an integrated fashion and not just as stage business. Allow the experience to come into the body and affect you (without forcing it). Treat this run-through as an improvisation (without changing the lines) for exploring the character's physicality. It's important that all the gestures, old and new, are done spontaneously—no planning to do a certain gesture at a certain point in the scene. During this run-through, you will discover the character's instincts and understand how you are enhancing your characterization with detailed physicality that makes this character more individual and unique. The gestures are the catalyst to help you discover the deep character.

Gestures provide access to a deeper or transformative level of character work, a level you may not have imagined, that surprises you with delight as you discover it. When Chris O'Dowd played Lennie to James Franco's George in a Broadway production of *Of Mice and Men*, he wowed the New York Times critic with his gesture work: "O'Dowd has mastered a small but refined repertoire of facial expressions and gestures (one hand movement has the delicacy of an artist) that is quite astonishing. Going beyond that physical expressiveness, the depth and understanding he brings to the role render Lennie, quite simply, heartbreaking."

The private gesture rehearsal usually takes about 20-30 minutes for up to six gestures. There is space in this methodology for personalization. However, unless you commit the new gestures to muscle memory by practicing them and then introducing them into a scene rehearsal, your finished work is likely to appear mechanical and manufactured instead of spontaneous.

WHEN YOU NEED TO

MAKE IT MORE QUIRKY

A director who asks that a character be quirkier usually feels the character isn't interesting or funny enough. You need to create a new character, but there may not be time. What can you do if there is no time or you have scenes in the can that cannot be replaced? Or the director just needs to make one scene more interesting or funnier?

A character sometimes needs to be quirky in a scene or scenes due to where he is on his character arc. Examples of appropriate character arcs include sloppy to respectful, repulsion to attraction, confusion to clarity, weakness to strength. The character might be quirky at the beginning of the arc. The quirkiness may diminish as the script proceeds or disappear suddenly and totally due to a story point late in the script.

★ Solution #1 — Physical Irritation

Pick a physical irritation that is temporarily tormenting your character. For example, your character has to sneeze but can't or doesn't want to, your character very much needs to go to the bathroom but doesn't want to leave the scene, your character is wearing an itchy bra or way too tight underwear, your character's foot has fallen asleep, or your character has flatulence.

During the scene for which the director has given the note, focus on the irritation and your attempts at relief, while disguising or hiding both the irritation and the relief attempts from others.

The degree of quirkiness will be determined by how much the irritation is bothering you or how much you succeed or fail at hiding the relief attempts. The relief attempts should involve your body (for example, shaking your head to deal with an ear irritation); the set (sliding up, down, or sideways on a chair to relieve a wedgie); the props (surreptitiously scratching an itch with any prop); or other characters (a handshake or embrace to maintain equilibrium).

An example of one actor's use of physical irritation can be seen in *The Mary Tyler Moore Show.* In an episode titled "Chuckles Bites the Dust," Mary is a mourner at the funeral of her TV station colleague the resident children's show host, Chuckles the Clown. In this scene, Mary suffers from inappropriate and uncontrollable laughter while the priest conducts the service. This is a great and hilarious example of a character having an irritation, failed attempts at relief, and covering up or camouflaging the attempts. The scene and the episode (*TV Guide* called it "The funniest single episode in the history of television comedy.") are easily seen on YouTube.

Adding the irritation and your attempts at relief ultimately might not be appropriate for performance. However, exploring it and improvising your relief attempts might lead you to a new sense of how your character takes care of herself—a big discovery that deepens your character and has the potential to locate the quirky side of the character.

Solution #2 — Desire for Invisibility

Make a secret choice that you will be fired if a specific character in your scene looks at you. If your character is an employee, it's your character who will be fired. If your character is not an employee, you (the actor) will be fired. Ideally, the status of the character whose look you must avoid should be higher than your character's status: for example, boss and employee or domineering wife (or mother-in-law) and timid husband. While playing the scene, focus on hiding or camouflaging yourself from this character. Take advantage of the props on hand and use them to hide yourself—for example, by holding in front of your face a menu, a napkin, a magazine, a book, a plate, or a scarf. Have fun improvising with the props in a way that makes some kind of sense for your character, especially when you use one prop after another. You will probably be seen, but you don't have to know your attempts failed. So you keep at it. Sometimes, you might only be trying to make yourself as small as possible. Other times, you might go as far as literally disappearing behind furniture or other large objects. Very quirky. If the director likes the direction this is going and tells you to do more or up the stakes, change being fired to something more severe. For example, you will be arrested and go to jail or you will have to commit suicide. You might even increase the number of characters in the scene you have to hide from.

★ Solution #3 — Attitude Line

Take on an attitude line for the scene in question. Examples of attitude lines that can provide quirkiness include: I'm enthusiastic; I mean well!; I'm funny; I'm a winner; I'm impulsive; I'm spontaneous; I must!; I'm outrageous; Why me?; I'm obsessive; I'm neurotic; I'm fussy; I'm anxious; I'm nervous, I'm a perfectionist; I'm childlike; I'm excited.

Your body as well as your mind must assume the attitude line. The simple process is detailed in Attitude Lines: Process and Archetypes [p. 9].

WHEN YOU NEED TO

CHANGE YOUR RELATIONSHIP STATUS

Sometimes the balance in your relationship with another character is off. There needs to be a stronger sense of which character has more power, or thinks they do. The power dynamic may be apparent in the script, dictated by the given circumstances. For example, the two characters have a professional relationship: boss / employee, military officer / private, teacher/student, doctor/patient. Or the power dynamic may not be so apparent. Or it may change as circumstances change. The characters could have a personal relationship: a dating, married, or divorced couple; ex-lovers; friends; neighbors; family members. You get this note when the director feels the characters are playing as equals, neither of them exhibiting a more or less powerful stance and attitude, or when one of you is exhibiting the proper status and the other is not (for example, both are playing high status instead of one high and one low). The director wants this balanced relationship changed to an unbalanced one. Another less likely possibility is that you are playing an unbalanced relationship and the director wants a balanced one. A balanced relationship, both high or both low, is frequently found in comedies.

All Solutions

If the characters are not supposed to have equal power, determine where the status imbalance should be. In a professional relationship, it is usually obvious—someone is in charge. In a personal relationship, it can be less obvious. You have to look to what's emotionally important to the characters. The character with the power with respect to that thing has the higher status. There are exceptions when deceit is involved, usually in comedies (*Tartuffe*,

Tootsie, The Inspector General, Dirty Rotten Scoundrels, Sullivan's Travels). In these situations, a low-status character can masquerade as a high-status character and vice versa. They can even go back and forth, raising and lowering their own and the others' status.

Determining a character's status is not necessarily about professional or social rank. It might be determined by how a character treats and is treated by others. It might be determined by the *expectation* of how a character treats and is treated by others. Sometimes the drama or comedy is a product of a character low in the social order treating others as if he has a high status. Or vice versa.

★ Solution #1 — Attitude Line

Prior to "Action" or before entering on stage, take on an appropriate attitude line [see Attitude Lines: Process and Archetypes, p. 9]. For a high-status character, select from: I know best, I'm in charge, I'm superior, I'm smarter, I'm important, I have integrity, I know it all, I'm confident, I'm in control, I'm entitled, I'm a winner, I'm calm, and (with an easy, graceful, and charming line reading) I have to. For the low-status character, select from: I'm determined, I mean well, I want more, I'm sensitive, I'm eager, I'm incompetent, I'm excited, I must!, I'm frustrated, I'm earnest, and (with an imperative line reading) I have to. To guide your choice, go through the script with this list in front of you, looking only at your lines, and see which attitude line is borne out by how your character speaks and what she says.

Solution #2 — As-If

Play the scene using an as-if relationship in which the participants have the appropriate status. For instance, to give the other character higher status, it's as if he is your boss and can have you fired at the drop of a hat; or he is smarter than you and is prone to ridiculing people who say dumb things. Choose details or circumstances of the as-if relationship that resonate with you and give you a visceral feeling of being inferior to someone. Make the other character the owner, in one way or another, of the location or setting of the scene and stay alert to a feeling of intruding on the other. If you are the high-status character, reverse the roles (you are the boss, the smarter one, etc.). You own the location of the scene, in one way or another, and the other is intruding. When making the choices for the as-if relationship, pay attention to the distance between the higher and lower status. If you choose, for example, an employee and a boss, is the boss a project supervisor, a foreman, or the CEO of a giant company? It's best to keep the distance minimal, which will allow you more flexibility in how the scene develops. On the other hand, if it's a comedy, explore a choice that has maximum distance.

Solution #3 — Substitution

For the other character in the scene, you can subtitute someone in your life, present or past, whose presence would trigger for you the required status, someone who would make you feel one down or one up. You could also substitute someone you have never met. For instance, if you need to feel one down, it could be Stephen Spielberg, someone you respect; if one up, it could be an incompetent co-worker to whom you feel superior. Simply play the scene and *substitute* in your mind that person for the other character.

While waiting for "Action" to be called, start visualizing the person you are substituting. The more detailed the visualization, the better. Keep narrowing the visualization—see the whole body, the whole face, then the nose, lips, eyes. Convince yourself that you are playing the scene with this person. Through visualization, transfer that face onto the face of the character you are playing the scene with. As the scene progresses, go with the feeling of the status difference. Let that feeling grow and dictate how you are playing the scene, especially line readings. In this way, you are *personalizing* something so that it has meaning for you and helps you attain the character's status as required by the director.

Solution #4 — Secret

Have a status secret, something unknown to the other characters (or actors) and the audience. It can be your character's secret or your own. A character's secret is better because it's more grounded as a part of your whole performance and may lead to interesting discoveries about your character or the script. A personal secret can suffice if you find it to be rich and stimulating. Regardless of whether you go personal or character, no one will ever know your secret except you. Here is an example of a character secret for when your scene partner has a higher status than you. You know that the other character is in a position to give you what your character wants. Here is a personal secret. After this acting job, the other actor is going to produce and direct a major film that has a lead role for which you are perfect. Here is an example of a character secret for when your scene partner has a lower status than you. You know that the other character is about to be arrested for some crime (the level of the crime affords you leeway for adjusting the status distance between you, for example, tax cheating vs. murder). Here is a personal secret. You know that the other actor will be fired as soon as the producer arrives on set. When playing the scene, have a high degree of awareness of the secret and your status attitude will adjust accordingly.

While focusing on the secret, allow your body to respond to it. Don't anticipate your body's physicalized response.

Solution #5 — Ladder Rehearsal

This rehearsal technique may be helpful. Play the scene on one or two stepladders. The higher status character stands on a higher step than the lower status character. Start with only one step between the characters and experiment with additional or fewer steps during and depending on your dialogue until you have the visceral feeling of the difference in your status. Stay open to responding to the spatial positioning with your whole body. Allow the steps between you to influence your character and how she relates to the other character.

Solution #6 — Deck of Cards

For immediate understanding of a relationship's status dynamics, assign playing cards to the other characters and yourself that match the status order of the characters. Who is a King? Who is a lowly Three?

Play the differences between the cards. How does the Seven behave toward the Ace? How does the Queen carry herself? Consider how you expect to be treated by the others. How does a Jack expect to be treated by an Eight? And vice versa?

Sometimes the drama or comedy is a product of a character low in the social order treating others as if he has a high status (a Four behaving as if he is an Ace). In some of these situations, there is actual deceit in play, such as in *The Dirty Dozen*, when Donald Sutherland, a condemned low-life criminal and a private in the army, impersonates an officer reviewing and inspecting the troops. In Gogol's *The Inspector General*, Khlestakhov, a young and impoverished clerk, assumes the role of the Inspector General and rips off the town. The opposite is also a possibility—an Ace behaving as if he is a Four. For example, in Preston Sturges' film *Sullivan's Travels*, a Hollywood director sets out to experience life as a homeless person in order to gain relevant life experience for his next movie.

WHEN YOU NEED TO

MAKE A DECISION ABOUT WHAT YOUR CHARACTER KNOWS

In preparation, in rehearsals, or on set, the director will often ask you (or you will ask yourself), "Does my character know_____?" For example, you might ask if your character knows that another character is lying to you, or if your character knows that this is the last time you will see him.

Solution

Always answer this question "Yes." You will make your character smarter, which is always a good thing. Whether you answer the question with a "Yes" or a "No," it doesn't change your dialogue. Answering with a "Yes" influences your character's thinking and how the dialogue is spoken. It influences your subtext. It will also influence your acting choices for that beat. Even if your character is supposed to be dumb, make him as smart as he can be within the givens of the script—his dialogue, his actions, his part of the whole. Making him as smart as possible enriches the role and makes him more interesting to the audience—as is the case for all characters. *"The character always knows"* is a useful mantra.

There are, however, some stories that depend on characters not knowing something. If knowing something disrupts or gives the lie to the plot or story, the right answer to a question about what your character knows might be "No." For example, if you are playing Othello, you might ask yourself, "Do I know that Iago is deceiving me to make me jealous?" If you answer "Yes," it changes the story and meaning of the play. In comedies, a vein of the humor is often the character's self-blindness, for example, Do I know that I am acting foolishly? Rebellious? Lying to myself? The answer might be "No." This is common in sitcoms—*Seinfeld*, *Friends*, and *Frasier*, for example. In Chekhov, frequently the joke is that a character is very perceptive about the inauthenticity of others, but totally clueless about herself.

WHEN YOU NEED TO

GET THE ROLE ON TRACK

The director thinks that parts of your performance are working, but the overall performance is not coming together and seems fragmented. Individual scenes are good enough but don't connect to one another. This situation occurs more in theater than camera productions. The difficulty in dealing with this note is determining whether the problem is essentially a character problem throughout all the scenes or an objective problem in one or more scenes.

Solution #1 — Objective Problem

An objective problem means that your objective choices for one or more scenes don't make sense in light of your character's objective for the whole script. The overall objective is called the *super-objective*—what your character wants to achieve by the end of the story (script), as opposed to what he may want to achieve in each scene. If your character's individual scene objectives are not conducive to his super-objective, your character is off track. You should know the character's super-objective—for example, catch the bad guy, be rich and powerful, be a good parent, get to Moscow, find the best mate, or discover the vaccine. Knowing your super-objective keeps you on track when determining your individual scene objectives and helps you spot when you have made a contradictory choice. If you get this note, review your objective choices for each scene, looking for choices not in service of your super-objective. If you find any, change them to fit your super-objective. If you don't find any, reconsider your super-objective choice. If you are confident in your choices for the super-objective and scene objectives and in your playing of these choices, you might have a character problem.

Solution #2 — Character Problem

Consider all your scenes and determine if you are dropping the character or changing the character in any of them. Asking the director will be helpful. If you have this problem, make sure to stay in your original character when doing these scenes. If dropping or changing the character is not the problem, ask the director if she feels your character doesn't work overall and you need a whole new one. If that's the case, review the components of how you created the character to find out where you went off track. Also, see Quickly Change to the Director's Vision of the Character [p. 191].

XI

LESS IS MORE

In his book *Acting in Film*, Michael Caine shares a story about the great film director George Cukor directing Jack Lemmon in his first film role. Jack kept doing a scene, and George kept saying, "Cut. Less, Jack, less." And Jack would do the scene again.

George: "Cut. Less, Jack, less."

And Jack would do it again.

George: "Cut. Less, Jack, less."

Jack finally said, "If I do any less, I'll be doing nothing."

George: "*Now* you've got it."

There are many occasions when you might receive a note asking you to do less of something. Unfortunately, the something is frequently vague. The lack of specificity can drive you nuts. You get notes that say take it down, simplify it, do less, just be yourself, don't act—you're enough. On the assumption that you are trusting the director's response, or you know on your own that something's off and you feel too big, too busy, or too effortful for your part of the whole, look in this section for the kind of note you are receiving from the director or for what's troubling you. There is a Chinese proverb that may not have been intended for this kind of problem but speaks to it: "Good fortune is as light as a feather and few are strong enough to carry it."

[Reminder: Many of the solutions throughout the book involve the **Secret Magic Stuff** that I find to be most effective with the quickest results. Those solutions are highlighted by a star ★.]

WHEN YOU NEED TO

TAKE IT DOWN

Ask the director to clarify what he wants taken down. Does he feel you are overacting? Not listening to the other characters? Making a wrong choice? Something else?

Solution #1 — Be Wary of Overacting

If he says, "It's too big" or "Don't let me know you're acting," keep all your choices and diminish their physical size and intensity. At the same time, increase your listening to the other characters. You might try adding business to the scene, specifically an activity with one or more props that requires your real attention to accomplish, such as putting on makeup, rolling a joint, preparing something, cleaning something. While saying your lines on cue, focus on the doing of the activity and not your other acting choices. If this doesn't work and the director says, "You need to take it down more," do the next take, rehearsal, or performance playing the scene with no business and heightening your concentration on listening [see Reflection Listening, p. 27]. If you frequently get the note that you are too big or overacting, the problem might not be that you're overacting, but that what you're doing is not coming out as authentic. To solve it, consider what the great director Sidney Lumet (five Academy Award nominations for Best Director), said to Cherry Jones (two Tonys and three Emmys) with respect to the fear that theater actors are too big for the camera and it comes out as overacting, "I know a lot of people who think theater actors are going to be over the top. I always tell actors from the theater that you can hang from the rafters and turn purple, as long as you mean it."

Solution #2 — Integrate More Listening and Looking

Regardless of your acting choices, make a point of integrating more moments of looking at and listening to the other characters. This is especially important if you have business—for example, getting dressed. If the director tells you to take it down more, do the next take, rehearsal, or performance playing the scene with no business and heightening your concentration on listening [see Reflection Listening, p. 27].

Solution #3 — Ask the Director Detailed Questions

Ask the director in what area he wants the change. Does he want you to do less, different, or no business? Different business means replace what you are now doing with something else less busy, such as, replace putting on your makeup with casually selecting a piece of jewelry. Less business means you should be selective and only do those parts of the business you feel are essential and lose everything else. Does he want a different intention? If so, review with the director what your choices are for your objective and what action you have been playing. If you know how to play an emotion, ask if he would like you to play a different emotion. If he gives you a specific answer about where he wants the different choice, make the change. If you don't know how to make that change, turn to the front of this book and look at the table of contents. If the director doesn't know what he wants and responds to your attempt at clarification with "Just take it down," use the above solution to *overacting*.

WHEN YOU NEED TO

TONE IT DOWN

What your character is feeling, his behavior toward other characters, and the stakes of the scene add up to the general or specific tone you bring to a scene. To tone it down means to diminish the intensity of this tone.

Solution #1 — Actions

Consider a less intense *action* verb for overcoming your obstacles and attaining your objective. For example, instead of "demand," choose "persuade." A different obstacle might be helpful, one that is easier to overcome. Or you can adjust your attitude toward your action and pick a less intense adverb. For example, "encourage enthusiastically" could be "encourage calmly."

★ Solution #2 — Emotions

Review your emotion choices and consider less intense emotions.

Solution #3 — Subtext and Stakes

If you are playing the scene with subtext, ask yourself whether it's necessary. If the scene doesn't need it, remove it. If the writer intended a subtext, consider lowering the stakes of the subtext you have been playing.

Solution #4 — Relationship

Are you placing too much emphasis on your relationship status with the other character? Reconsider your choices and place your focus on an aspect of the scene other than the relationship.

Solution #5 — Your Part of the Whole

Consider the rhythms, volume, and energy you are bringing to the scene. Are you racing through the scene? Slow it down. Are you playing to the back of the house even though it's camera acting? Adjust, confident that knowing how to play big onstage makes it easier to underplay on camera. Are you overpowering the other actors? Be a more compatible part of the whole scene.

Solution #6 — Variety

If you are playing your part of the scene in one tone (nostalgic memory, tragedy, anger, or love), the note to tone it down may mean the director would rather you play the individual beats and moments with different choices and spontaneity rather than a monochromatic tone. Find a more dynamic approach with more variety.

WHEN YOU NEED TO

RELAX AND SIMPLIFY

Sometimes this note reads "You are enough." It might mean he's seeing tension where none should be. It might mean he feels you are trying to accomplish too much with your acting choices and are losing the essential part of the scene. Sometimes this note just means your acting is too big and coming out phony. If the scene involves subtext, you might be too deeply involved in playing the subtext and the surface scene is suffering. Sometimes directors don't know what to say to remedy what they feel needs fixing, or they don't know what's not working. If "relax and simplify" is the only feedback you are getting, you can respond with Solutions #1 or #2 below or ask the director for more feedback to help you solve the problem most fruitfully.

Ask him if he's seeing tension. If so, where? Does your performance seem complicated? If he answers yes, ask in what way. Can he give you any hints as to what's specifically provoking his note? Where does he think you are going off? Get the director to be as specific as possible. If you are shooting, stay mindful of the time constrictions and don't turn a quick chat into a time-consuming discussion. You can do that after you become a star.

★ Solution #1 — Commit to the Moment

Let go of your choices. Focus on being relaxed and approach the scene as if it's a final level of a repeat exercise, listening and speaking in the moment. If you have difficulty with relaxing and you don't have a favorite relaxation technique, try the 40-breath relaxation process presented in Deal with Being Nervous, Solution #1—Get Present [p. 185].

★ Solution #2 — Reflection Listening

You can simplify what you are doing and lose any tension by dropping all your acting choices and directing all your concentration toward heightened listening. Use the process outlined in Reflection Listening [p. 27].

★ Solution #3 — Horizontal (diaphragm) Breathing

Horizontal or diaphragmatic breathing is more conducive to calmness. Do the horizontal breathing process found in Deal with Being Nervous, Solution #4 [p. 187].

WHEN YOU NEED TO

JUST TALK AND LISTEN

The director doesn't like something you are doing, but this note, sometimes given after you've tried to make adjustments that did not work, does not say exactly what's wrong. Instead of obsessing over what it might be, ask her. Perhaps her answer will ring a bell. If so, ask for one more take before you "just talk and listen." If she says "no," or the extra take doesn't solve the problem, it's now time to just talk and listen.

Solution #1 — Follow Your Impulses

Other than being in character; drop all your acting choices. While focusing on your scene partner, listen and speak spontaneously with no preparation. In other words, follow your impulses. If you are familiar with all the levels of the Repetition Exercise from your acting class, what you are doing here is the same as the final level.

★ Solution #2 — Reflection Listening

Heighten your listening and increase the communion between you and your scene partner with Reflection Listening [p. 27].

WHEN YOU NEED TO

STOP ACTING!

Sometimes you are told, "You're acting," or "Don't act."

Solution

Please see: Take it Down [p. 215, the section on overacting]; Just Talk and Listen, Solution #1 [p. 221]; Relax and Simplify, Solution #1 [p. 219].

WHEN YOU NEED TO

JUST BE YOURSELF — NO CHARACTER!

This note is uncommon in the theater, where the character grows and evolves in rehearsal under the director's eye. In film and TV, however, the director may not see what you are doing with the character until your first day of shooting. The director may just want the actor he cast, not the character the actor created on his own. Regardless of why you were cast, receiving this note to just be yourself can be troublesome for many actors, especially after devoting time and work to creating a character. Be myself? Who am I? What part of me is the director referring to? Sylvester Stallone, after eight *Rocky* movies and five for *Rambo,* says, "The hardest thing in acting is to be yourself."

★ Solution #1 — Attitude Line

A very simple and fast way to "just be yourself" instead of the character you created is to take on a particular and special attitude line of two words: I am. The process for taking on an attitude line is presented in Attitude Line Process [p. 13]. In that process, when you are picking the line reading for "I am," it should be calm, peaceful, centered, and neutral (not "I am!!"). At the end of the preparation process (about five minutes), the character the director didn't like will be completely gone, replaced by you being you. Every human being is himself and no one else. An extra bonus is that you will also feel empowered, strong, calm, confident, assured, and even proud to be, uniquely, yourself.

Return to the set and retain this body feeling. You can refresh it instantly by saying to yourself "I am" whenever you feel the need to do so. Always allow your body to respond when you refresh.

The character is now based on who you are, and despite losing the character you originally created, you can still play your original acting choices for the scene—for example, emotions, objectives, and actions. Be open to changing the choices if they no longer fit. Don't do anything that will take you back to the previous character.

★ Solution #2 — Reflection Listening

For an immediate and quick disposal of the character, play the scene focused on Reflection Listening [p. 27]. This approach will help you out when you can't take the five-minute break to prepare your "I am" Attitude Line. However, Reflection Listening is a quick fix for what you are shooting right now and won't serve you well if you plan on using it for multiple scenes. At the first opportunity, do the Attitude Line process from Solution #1.

XII

MORE IS MORE

A major difference between theater and camera acting is that, in the theater, when you give a performance you give a performance, whereas, in camera acting, when they call "Action" you do a rehearsal. In the theater, you work out your part in rehearsals and play it in performance; in camera acting, every take is still working out your part. When working out your part, whether it's in rehearsal or during a take, there are times when you need extra technique to assist you in solving particular problems with confidence. Bobby Lewis, an important teacher of acting and directing and the author of *Method or Madness*, was fond of quoting Edgar Degas: "If you have 100,000 francs' worth of skill, spend another five sous to buy more."

[Reminder: Many of the solutions throughout the book involve the **Secret Magic Stuff** that I find to be most effective with the quickest results. Those solutions are highlighted by a star ★.]

WHEN YOU NEED TO

BE IN THE MIDDLE OF THE SCENE WHEN "ACTION" IS CALLED

Despite the phrase "middle of the scene," this note has nothing to do with what part of the scene you are shooting (beginning, middle, or end). The note means you are still preparing for the shot after the shot has started. If you were a pitcher on a baseball team, you would be winding up to throw the ball, when all we want to see is the pitch. If you were a card player, you would be considering what to discard, when all we want to see is the card leaving your hand. Sometimes this preparation takes the form of a long pause while you prepare inwardly, or a deep breath to eliminate tension and center yourself. The director wants you a little further along when "Action" is called. At other times, the note might be "You need *the moment before*." This note concerns the opposite effect from the one above. The director is pointing out that you are starting the shot too abruptly or too cold. What you are doing carries too little sense of what has led up to the beginning of the shot.

Solution #1 — Run the Scene

While waiting for "Action" to be called, run the scene with your scene partner(s) up to where the "Action" cue will come, so you are firing on all cylinders when the director calls "Action."

Solution #2 — Pre-Scene Improv

If the shot is at the beginning of a scene, engage your scene partner, if he is willing, to improvise with you what's happening and spoken up to the moment of "Action." Assume that where the writer starts the scene is the middle of the scene. At "Action," continue with the real scene as written. This is called a Pre-Scene Improv. There are multiple approaches to choose from for the improvisation [see the next entry, Do a Pre-Scene Improv, p. 229].

Solution #3 — Actions

If your scene partner declines improvising a pre scene with you, prior to "Action," you can silently focus on playing your action verb, or even say it out loud and articulate what you are going to do ("I'm seducing you" or "I'm going to seduce you"). Or you can improvise without your partner's participation by playing your action choice and improvising lines silently or out loud supporting that choice as you wait for your "Action" cue.

Solution #4 — Play Your Choices

Start playing your acting choice for the scene in anticipation of "Action." You don't have to limit yourself to playing actions and objectives. You can refresh your acting choice at "Action." Examples of acting choices that can be initiated while waiting for "Action" include physicalizing your emotion or attitude, making your subtext more vivid to yourself, tightening your conflict issue and keeping it taut, or refreshing your attitude line.

WHEN YOU NEED TO

DO A PRE-SCENE IMPROV

In camera acting, some directors ask for—and some actors prefer—an improv leading up to the start of the scene in order to begin the shot fully there and in the moment. A pre-scene improvisation is used as a warm-up. The goal is to capture the characters as if they are in the middle of a scene instead of at the beginning. A pre-scene improv can also lead to discoveries that pay off during the shot or later in the scene. In rehearsals for the theater, directors use pre-scene improvs for the same reason, to explore what's needed for a scene to begin as if the actors are in the middle of it.

Solution #1 — Fill In the Blanks

What if the writer could provide you with a beat of dialogue or, perhaps, another story element preceding the written scene? What would you need or want that additional pre-scene beat to accomplish? If you can answer this question, you can provide the words yourself, in character, during the pre-scene improv leading up to the moment of "Action."

Solution #2 — The Objective

In character, respecting your intention, improvise dialogue about your problem or objective—what you want in the scene. However the other character responds to you, use what she says to go further in your improvised dialogue about what you want. You should feel that you are in charge of your objective. Stay in character and, like an athlete, push off with intention and power. If talking about your objective makes you feel self-conscious, avoid this solution. On the other hand, talking about it may help you to relax and stay open to new ideas to verbalize.

Solution #3 — Play Your Action

In character, focus on playing the action you have selected for the actual beginning of the scene. Have a clear purpose, the objective (what you want in the scene), and go after it with your action choice. Improvise dialogue to support the action. Let's say your objective is to get the other character to break up with you, and your action is to patronize. Whatever you improvise, make sure that you are patronizing your scene partner. You are free to improvise dialogue that may or may not include specifying or hinting at the objective. If talking about your objective makes you feel self-conscious, avoid mentioning it. On the other hand, talking about it may help you to relax and stay open to new ideas to verbalize. Stay alert to see how the other character is responding to your action and improvised dialogue. Is she thwarting you, or do her responses suggest the possibility of success for you? You may have an opportunity to make adjustments as the pre-scene improv continues. This solution can be done without dialogue by combining it with Solution #5, Improv Without Dialogue or Solution #4, Subtext.

Pay attention to how your body feels and behaves during the pre-scene improv. That's the physicalization that accompanies your action. Maintain that physicalization when you go into the actual scene and continue to play your action.

Solution #4 — Subtext

For preparation, ask and answer these questions: Is there anything you can't talk about in the scene? Is the scene about something that is not mentioned or referred to in the dialogue? If so, warm up by focusing on what you can't talk about and commence the improv by staying in character and going out of your way to talk around it while it's all you can think about. Your improv dialogue is a cover for what you can't talk about; it has the same subtext as the scene.

OR: Stay in character and elevate the subtext into the improvised dialogue by talking about what you can't talk about in the actual scene. At "Action," you're still thinking about it but can no longer talk about it, so it immediately becomes the subtext for the scene's dialogue.

Using the scene's subtext for the pre-scene improv can be combined with Solution #3, Play your Action.

★ Solution #5 — Improv Without Dialogue

Use the set and props to improvise in the physical world of the characters. Elia Kazan said, "I always try to move actors through scenery, not in front of it, so they actually touch things. If they're in front of everything, the scenery might as well be a painted backdrop." Take the freedom during the pre-scene improv to move around the set. Give yourself (in character) the task of making physical contact with different set pieces and props, using them in some fashion. Examples might include: discovering a clock and setting the correct time; taking a cup of coffee from an urn; looking for something in drawers and cabinets. For the sake of spontaneity and potential for discoveries, improvise this task in the moment. If you don't have the freedom of movement and must stay on your mark, do an activity with a prop within your reach. Examples might include: repairing or attempting to repair something; applying makeup; rolling a joint. If there are no props within your reach, have a prop in your costume (for example, your pocket) and do an activity with it. With this approach, you can start your scripted dialogue whenever the director calls "Action." Don't assume you can't move around the set during the pre-scene improv. The camera hasn't been turned on yet. Just end the improv on your mark. In a rehearsal off set, use space set pieces and props. If the stage manager has provided real essential props, don't limit yourself to only using them. You might discover a new space prop that will then be deemed essential and added to the prop list. My student Malcolm-Jamal Warner relates: "When we are rehearsing scenes for my show, *Malcolm & Eddie*, I'm always improvising activity and discovering objects (space objects) and at the end of the rehearsal, the prop people ask me what props I want. I think about what I used (in space) that I liked and then I tell them those. And they get them for the next rehearsal or shooting."

Avoid activities requiring reading. What you read or pretend to read puts you in your head and takes you out of the scene, while activities that require physical doing take you out of your head and create potential for experimenting and discovering whole new moments, feelings, and thoughts.

★ Solution #6 — Gibberish

Gibberish is the substitution of a nonsense language for a real language, replacing real words with any made-up nonsense words or accumulation of vocal sounds. Instead of improvising pre-scene dialogue, run the actual scene in gibberish and, at "Action," restart the scene in English, staying open to any impact the gibberish may have had on you in the pre-scene improv. Gibberish is an excellent warm-up and may surprise you by how it can improve the actual scene: increased physical freedom and spontaneity; lack of self-consciousness; the experience of doing without thinking; better connection with more going on between characters; new relationship discoveries; stronger needs, hurts, and other emotions; higher stakes; more energy; clarification of the writer's intent; discovery of new levels without effort; the experience of being totally in the moment; and the elimination of misguided, preconceived notions about the scene.

If you are new to using gibberish, you may have to do it a few times to be comfortable with improvising in it. Unless you know that your scene partner relishes taking risks in their acting, it's probably best to alert your scene partner prior to doing it. You can say that you will do your lines in gibberish and invite them to join you or do their lines in English.

Solution #7 — Relationship

Use the pre-scene improv to establish, explore, or highlight your character's relationship to the other character.

Raise or Lower Your Status

If the scene is about a status imbalance where one character has more or less standing or power than the other, or think they do, use the information and solutions found in Change Your Relationship Status [p. 202] to approach your pre-scene improv. After determining that a status imbalance exists and who is high and low, do a pre-scene improv using one of those solutions. While those solutions apply to the performance or rehearsal of an actual scene, they are also easily used to approach a pre-scene improv. If the characters are equal in status, a status pre-scene improv is not the best approach.

Attitude Line

Take the opportunity of the pre-scene improv to refresh your character's attitude line [see Attitude Line Process, p. 13]. For the pre-scene improv, focus on maintaining the attitude line throughout your body and improvise without ever saying your attitude line out loud. If you let the attitude line fuel your inside and outside, you will know what to do in the moment. It will be easy to spontaneously improvise with control as you: (1) respond to whatever your scene partner says or does; or (2) depending on your impulse in the moment, take charge of the pre-scene improv, leading your scene partner in the direction you want to go (pursuing your objective, doing an activity, or playing your status relationship). Staying focused on your attitude line and holding it throughout your body will reinforce your characterization and provide you with intention and power as you leave the pre-scene improv and go into the scene.

★ Solution #8 — Happy

If the scene needs to start with the characters in a happy and jovial state, for the pre-scene improv, play the theater game *Yes! And . . .* In character, respond to everything your scene partner says in the improv by saying "Yes! And . . . " and improvise the rest of that sentence. It's best to say "Yes! And . . ." with enthusiasm. As the improv continues, build on your own and each other's enthusiasm. Go with it! Before starting, it is advisable to alert your scene partner to what you are going to do. Invite him to join you in the game. If he declines, you can still play it by responding to his improvised lines with "Yes! And . . ."

★ Solution #9 — Tension, Anger, Argument, or Conflict

If the scene needs to start with the characters in tension with each other or in the middle of a conflict, isolate the source of the tension or conflict by stating it as the confrontation of two opposing wants (She: I want my mom to live with us. He: I want your mom to go to an old folks home.). Imagine a rope with one end tied around your waist and the other end tied around the waist of the other character. The rope is tautly stretched between you. This rope represents the conflict. Each character is going to pull on his or her end of the rope without using their hands, creating a tug-of-war between you. Each character is to keep the rope taut at all times, pulling on it with your whole body to win the tug-of-war. Pulling the rope is accomplished by steadily increasing the tension in your body as you pull the imaginary rope (without your hands) and increasing the strength of your dialogue. You can increasingly strengthen your dialogue by building intensity, heightening volume, and, if possible, accelerating your ideas. In other words, as the improv proceeds, every time you speak, top your opponent with more strength. As in a real tug-of-war, the goal is to pull the other to your side—that is, win the conflict and get what you want. Wage the conflict with tension and confrontation, not rationality. This is not a time to remember you catch more flies with honey than vinegar. This improv is about getting what you want through confrontation.

There are two ways to approach the improv: spoken or disguised.

In the spoken approach, there are no conditions or rules, other than always keeping the rope taut and playing to win. You may improvise any dialogue at all in service of winning. In the disguised approach, you still have to keep the rope taut and play to win, but you must not mention or in any way reveal the conflict's opposing wants—even though it is the only thing on your mind. Your improvised conflict dialogue may be about anything else, a disguise for what you are really arguing about. Coming up with disguised conflict dialogue will not be difficult because whatever you say will suffice as long as you are focused on pulling on the rope with your body and voice and playing to win. With the disguised approach, the conflict's opposing wants become the subtext. If the actual scene begins with a disguised conflict, then you should apply the disguised conflict approach to the pre-scene improv. Either the spoken or the disguised approach will take you to the start of the real scene in tension with each other or in the middle of a conflict. At "Action," when the scripted scene starts, keep pulling that rope and stay in character! For this solution, you will need the participation of your scene partner to oppose you in the tug-of-war.

★ Solution #10 — Respect, Affection, or Love

If the scene needs to start with the characters attentive to and respectful of each other, for the pre-scene improv, improvise in character dialogue on any subject, from the script or not, while playing Reflection Listening [p. 27]. At "Action," start the scripted scene and stay open to any impact the pre-scene improv has had on you. You may discover the actual scene impacted by a better connection between you, with more going on—new relationship discoveries, higher stakes, and the experience of being totally in the moment in tandem with your scene partner. An alternative approach to improvising dialogue is to run the actual scene's dialogue while playing Reflection Listening. When "Action" is called, restart the scene and drop the Reflection Listening rules, staying open to any impact playing Reflection Listening may have had on you in the pre-scene.

If the characters are in love with each other and the scene's purpose is to show that, use this solution.

Solution #11 — Paraphrase

In your own words (not the writer's), improvise the gist of the scene you are about to do. At "Action," restart the scene with the scripted words. You will be able to say the dialogue in a way that may be more comfortable for you. Stay in character; it is easy to lose the tongue of the character when improvising the gist of the scene. At "Action," make sure you are fully in character as you restart the scene with the actual dialogue.

All Solutions

While keeping to the game plan of your chosen solution, always follow your impulses.

Doing a pre-scene improvisation is unlike rehearsal improvisations for many reasons I won't go into here. Suffice to say that a director encouraging rehearsal improvisation is allocating time for it, but there is very little time for it on a shooting set. A pre-scene improv is also unlike improvising in improv theater or comedy improv because you don't have to be concerned with narrative, comedic structure, or simply getting a laugh. The pre-scene improv is a warm-up for a specific scene in which the narrative and dialogue are already in place. In comedies, if a director encourages improvisation on a shooting set, those improvs have a different purpose than a pre-scene improv. Your comedic improv skills will pay off. When Robin Williams was working out in my class at the Spolin Theater Game Center in Hollywood in 1978 before *Mork & Mindy* began airing, he said to me, "I was expecting this class to be similar to other improv classes, but I was wrong. Instead, it's a fine acting class and I have to get the laughs without ad-libbing any shtick. This should really help if I get cast in movies." Little did we know that once movie directors experienced working with Robin, they would encourage him to go for it and take a shot at improvising and embellishing his scenes with his comedic genius.

All of the solutions provide you with something to do—physical, mental, or vocal. When you are fully focused on something you are doing, you are in the moment and not concerned with what to say next; the solutions will lead you through the pre-scene improv and prevent you from being distracted or flummoxed with the question "What do I say now?"

WHEN YOU NEED TO

GIVE IT MORE ENERGY

A director's note asking you to give your performance more energy probably means what you are doing is passive or casual, which might be all right for real life, but not for a performance (camera or stage). The director wants more aliveness, more presence. You need to bring your boldest self to the performance. You might be able to fix the problem by just waking up and heightening your performance in the next take or rehearsal.

Solution

You may need to look at how you are playing your choices. Are you playing them clearly and strongly? Evaluate honestly. If you spot a weakness, fix it. If you feel you are clearly and strongly playing your choices, you have to change a choice or two to something more active. For example, can your action be stronger? Can you suspect instead of consider, accuse instead of suspect, confront instead of accuse? If you are playing emotion choices, should the emotions be more intense? Nervous instead of concerned, scared instead of nervous, terrified instead of scared? Your character choice is probably not the issue here, because you would have heard about it before now. If the scene features a conflict, pull on your end of the conflict harder. Make sure you are playing to win the conflict and not just to not lose. If you decide your subtext choice can bring more energy, up the stakes of this choice and focus intensely on it while playing the beat or scene [see Play the Subtext, p. 100]. Use your subtext to make sure the scene is about more than what it appears to be about. If the writer chose to shape this beat or scene around the subtext and you play the subtext strongly, the energy level will go up.

WHEN YOU NEED TO

FILL THAT PAUSE

The director, or you, wants you to pause at a particular moment. You pause, and she points out that you are not filling the pause. She means the pause appears arbitrary, not justified by something in the character's inner life. The audience knows you're pausing for dramatic effect.

★ Solution #1 — Emotional Choreography

The most dynamic filling of a pause is emotional choreography. The audience sees you start the pause with one feeling and end it with another. The transitional moment between the two feelings happens during the pause and is compelling to watch. The first emotion is whatever emotion you are playing during the dialogue before the pause. During the pause, you make the Emotion Switch [Make a Sharp Transition from One Emotion to Another, p. 141] to the emotion you will play after the pause. If your scene breakdown or game plan doesn't provide a second emotion (in other words, you have chosen the dialogue before and after the pause to be in one beat), you will now have to make the dialogue after the pause the start of a new beat with its own emotion choice, or the start of a beat that has a non-emotion choice such as playing conflict or agreement or the beginning of a new action. If there is a scripted stage direction for the pause, as opposed to a director's or actor's invention, you can be pretty sure that the writer intended for there to be one emotion before the pause and another after it. If there is no scripted stage direction for the pause, your acting, because of your choice of switching emotions in the pause, will improve the writing without changing a word of the script.

Solution #2 — Action Switch

If you choose to not play emotions, a variation on Solution #1 would be to change your intention, objective, problem, or action in the pause. This action switch could make the switch as dynamic as emotional choreography. You might have to experiment with different actions to find the right one. An Emotion Switch is preferable because you don't have to rely on the uncertainty of which emotion will show up while playing different actions. As in Solution #1, the dialogue that follows the pause is now part of a new beat whose action is started in the middle of the pause. Go into the pause playing one action and end it playing another. Consider the pause to be a bridge between the two choices. The switch can occur at any time on the bridge, i.e., during the pause.

Solution #3 — Motivation

Motivate the pause. What's going on in your character's inner life? Does your character begin the pause because he needs a moment to think about what to do or say next? Does your character finish the line and now have a new idea that requires pausing to understand it, clarify it, or consider its ramifications? Does the new idea entail a change in your intention, so you must begin playing that new intention by the end of the pause? Or, as you approach the pause, does your character have second thoughts about what he is saying? During the pause, he reassures himself and continues with the next line. Maybe he not only continues but does so with even more conviction. If the dialogue after the pause changes direction from before the pause, that's because of what your character decides during the pause. Always think about what might be the reason for the pause. Ask yourself what the benefit is for your character in taking the pause. What might change coming out of the pause? Think of the pause as a bridge to what is new at the end of it. What are you doing while going across that bridge? If you can't find any benefit or reasonable motivation in the pause, cutting it might be a better choice. A sure way to lose the audience's attention is a pause in which nothing happens.

Solution #4 — Add Business

You might try adding business during the pause. Start or return to an activity with one or more props. It should be an activity that requires your real attention to accomplish, such as putting on makeup or making a cocktail. However long or short the pause, when you complete it and resume your dialogue, you may stop the activity or continue it during the dialogue. You can also combine this solution with any of the other solutions.

WHEN YOU NEED TO

COMMIT TO THE MOMENT

Some directors will give this note when they feel your performance is fading at a particular moment or section(s).

Solution #1 — Actions

If you rely on traditional acting, that is, pursuing you action to achieve your objective, pour some fuel on the fire and at the designated moments or sections heighten your commitment to playing your action there and play it stronger. Consider changing your action to a stronger and more active verb choice. Go for it. Get what you want! "Be bold, and mighty forces will come to your aid!" Or, as my students like to point out, "Go big or go home!"

Solution #2 — Story Point

Consider that the designated section(s) are not about going after what you want or justifying your point of view. Review these moments or sections to see if this is the case. If it is, you will frequently find that a story point has just occurred (within two or so pages of the designated moment). A story point is an event or dialogue that is significant to moving the plot forward, taking it in another direction, raising the stakes, or speeding it up. You must make a choice at every story point that concerns your character. What is your character's response to that story point? If you have not been playing that choice, you have found the cause of your problem, and it is easy to rectify by now playing that choice. For more on story points and responses, see Play the Story [p. 97]. In short, if you are playing an action or choosing a new action, play it boldly. If you are playing a story point response and it's an emotion, physicalize it [see Physicalizing an Emotion, p. 31]. If it's an attitude, either physicalize it or turn it into an attitude line [Attitude Line Process, p. 13] and physicalize that.

Both Solutions

Regardless of your approach to committing to the moment, continue to listen to the other characters and spontaneously integrate what you see and hear into what you are doing and saying. You might have received the note to commit to the moment because the director sees you anticipating what's going to happen instead of being authentically surprised by it. Michael Caine points out that "Anticipation is the enemy of all actors. It wreaks particularly savage havoc in films because the camera sees *everything,* especially lack of spontaneity."

WHEN YOU NEED TO

NAIL A CLOSE-UP (LISTENING)

Michael Caine said, "One of the most crucial jobs you'll have as an actor will be to know what you're thinking when you're not talking.... Oddly enough, your mind should work even *harder* in a close-up than it does during other shots because in the close-up, the performance is all in your eyes; you can't use the rest of your body to express yourself."

Preparing for a listening close-up starts with deciding whether your character is listening attentively or listening while thinking about other things or alternating between the two. Sometimes the director wants no reaction at all.

★ Solution #1 — Listening Attentively

There is a difference between listening politely and listening attentively.

Listening politely means listening courteously with no authentic investment in what is being said. Listening attentively means listening in the moment with your undivided attention and authentic respect for the speaker and what she has to say. To achieve the latter in a fashion that will command the audience's attention during your listening close-up, use an actor's tool called Reflection Listening. It is easily learned in a two-part exercise that takes less than 10 minutes and can be found in Reflection Listening [p. 27].

★ Solution #2 — Listening While Thinking About Other Things

Whether on camera or stage, spontaneously thinking the character's own thoughts while listening to another character is accomplished with a tool called Question and Answer Railroad

Tracks [see p. 3]. The audience will not know what you are thinking, but they will know that you are thinking real thoughts. Use this tool during the close-up to look like you are listening while there is something else going on (which there is). In addition to having an active doing process or focus that's compelling to watch during your listening close-up, you will discover how your character thinks and what they are thinking about with only a few improvised questions and answers. Question and Answer Railroad Tracks is a great way to get into thinking *as* the character instead of *for* the character. When the questions and answers lead you to a surprising discovery or a significant turn from one feeling to another, that take will not be cut. You also have an opportunity to highlight discoveries and emotional or attitudinal turns. Without changing what's going on inside you, just add a change of your focal spot. Don't move your head, just your eyes. For instance, think of your field of vision as a clock and your starting focal spot on the other character as the center of the clock's face. When you want to highlight a change in your inner life due to something you discover on the railroad tracks, let your eyes shift from the clock's center to the 3. You can then switch back at the next turn or shift your eyes from the 3 to the 6 or anywhere but the 3. The eye movement is dynamic and can provide the action in your close-up that editors and directors relish. This tool is very useful when the other character has a monologue. For more information on making turns see Railroad Tracks Turns [p. 6].

If the scene is dependent on a specific subtext [see Play the Subtext, p. 100], you can play the subtext and be thinking about other things while you appear to be listening politely. If the scene is not dependent on a specific subtext, Question and Answer Railroad Tracks is recommended.

★ Solution #3 — Alternating Listening Attentively with Listening While Thinking About Other Things

Switching between these two approaches to listening can be very dynamic. Start by listening attentively (Reflection Listening). When the other character says something that gets you to start thinking about other things, switch to Question and Answer Railroad Tracks. The director/editor will then have the opportunity to highlight the importance to your character of something the other character says. For example, if the other character reveals something important, the revelation is your cue to start thinking about what you are going to do with this new information. You can also make the opposite switch, going from listening while thinking about other things to listening with your full attention (Reflection Listening). Whichever way you choose to employ this switch, the moment of the switch will probably not be cut.

Switches between listening attentively and while thinking about other things can also be accomplished by taking advantage of your personal technique, such as changing from one emotion to another, changing from one action to another, or doing anything that prompts a different feeling. The transitional moment between the two feelings happens during the close-up and is compelling to watch. Elia Kazan said, "The best close-ups are pictorial records of a change from one attitude to another. They show a transition from one emotion to another." Your cues for the change can come out of something you hear while reflection listening or from something you discover while going down your question and answer railroad tracks. Kazan continues: "You see a man feeling or doing or about to do something. Instead, he changes his mind and starts to do something else. Or you see a man not notice something and suddenly he notices it. You see a man start to run away with fear, and instead he decides to move in and face what's scaring him. These transitions are when close-ups are at their best."

Solution #4 — Listening Without Reacting

A director will sometimes want you to have a blank face so the audience can project onto you what they think you are thinking and feeling. Pick a focal spot on the other character's face (nose, eyebrow, ear, etc.). As you look at that spot, focus on your breathing. Inhale and exhale through the nose to a controlled count. The count should be comfortable for you, probably two to four seconds. Keep repeating until "Cut." The size of the breaths should not be noticeable to the camera or audience. You should appear to be breathing normally.

WHEN YOU NEED TO

LISTEN TO A MONOLOGUE IN A COMPELLING FASHION

The solutions for Nail a Close-Up (Listening), [p. 246], can be applied to Listen to a Monologue in a Compelling Fashion.

WHEN YOU NEED TO

NAIL A CLOSE-UP (SPEAKING)

Making your speaking close-up dynamic with a sense of movement is the surest way to nail it.

★ Solution #1 — Switching Emotions

Start the shot in one emotional or attitudinal place and end it in another. The switch between the two provides the movement necessary for a dynamic shot.

Divide the scripted length of the shot into beats based on emotional changes. Label the beats with the emotion you think the writer intended for your character. Consider the given circumstances and use the text, including any stage directions, as clues to determining these choices.

Even though the close-up is on your face, physicalize the emotion choice with your whole body. At the cue where you have marked a beat change, do an Emotion Switch and completely change your body's physicalization to the emotion you have selected for the next beat [see Make a Sharp Transition from One Emotion to Another, p. 141]. A total switch in a split second is usually the most dynamic. Sometimes, by your design, the switch is gradual. For further information about physicalizing an emotion, see Play a Specific Emotion, Solution #1 [p. 132] and Physicalizing an Emotion [p. 31]. Continue to use the whole body to physicalize the emotion. You might wonder why you need to physicalize the emotion with your whole body if only part of your body (your face, for example) can be seen in a close-up. The reason is that the emotion will not be authentic if you are only indicating it with your face. As Michael Caine said, "You can't use your body to express yourself" in a close-up, but your whole body must support and complete the physicalization of the emotions you express on your face. In other words, when the close-up is on your face, bring your body along.

Solution #2 — Action Changes

Another way to make the shot dynamic with a sense of movement is to start the shot doing one action and end the shot doing another. The transitions between the beats provide the compelling movement during your close-up.

Divide the scripted length of the shot into beats based on action changes. Each beat gets a different verb that will overcome your obstacle(s) toward getting what you want. When performing, play the verb choices with transitions at the beat changes. When making the choices ahead of time, check that each choice is a viable possibility for overcoming the obstacle(s) and solving your problem. A total change of your action in a split second usually makes for the most dynamic close-up. Sometimes, by your design, the switch is gradual.

★ Solution #3 — Intensify Emotion

If you feel there are no beat changes in the shot, choose the emotion you think the writer intended the character to be feeling. Before "Action," physicalize the emotion choice with your whole body (not only your face!). After "Action" and for the length of the shot, keep heightening the physicalization with your whole body. In addition to intensifying the emotion, you will also be creating an emotion arc [see Intensify an Emotion Instead of Flatlining, p. 147, and Emotion Arc, p. 51]. The intensification is what gives the shot movement. How much you intensify and at what rate of speed are interpretive choices and are frequently discovered in the moment. A close-up on you will probably not be a very lengthy shot, so the intensification will probably be slight—for example, pleased to amused. But the intensification could potentially be stark—for example, irritated to furious. Arcing the emotion also makes it easier for the director to give you a note, such as "I need you to get much more frightened." On the next take, heighten your physicalization further, extending the arc to fulfill the director's note. If the other characters speak during your close-up, make sure you hear their dialogue and integrate it into the heightening of your emotion. During this process, do not try to hold onto any previous choices, including favorite line readings. Instead, just focus on doing the emotion arc and saying your lines on cue. Let your body supply the line readings spontaneously.

★ Solution #4 — Improvise

Rephrase what you want in the scene (the problem or objective) into a question that starts with the phrase "What to do with . . . ?" For example, if your objective is "I want to make love to her" and your obstacle is "She's married" and your action choice is "Seduce," you complete the question as follows: "What to do with *her*?" After you have the complete question, know that your answer to that question is your action choice, for example, seduce. You're ready to go: Prior to the shot and during it, in your mind, *frequently* ask yourself the question *"What to do with her?"* Every time you ask the question, treat it as if you have never asked or even considered it before. Then discover, for the first time (as if it's a brand-new idea), your answer, seduce her. Immediately, in the moment, do that—seduce her. Repeat the process often, asking yourself the question *"What to do with her?"* always as if it's the first time you have ever asked this question. Then discover, always for the first time, your answer: Seduce her. Repeating the answer to yourself every time you ask the question will spontaneously propel you in the moment to improvise methods of seduction. The moment you receive inspiration for determining the method and begin to employ it is what nails the close-up. The question and answer only change when you begin a new beat with both a new problem and action or with the same problem but with a new action. Here's another example. If your problem is *"I want stimulation"* and your obstacle is familiarity of the others and the surroundings and your action choice is "Stir things up," you complete the question as follows: *"What to do with everyone and everything?"* After you have completed the question, know that your answer is your action choice: *Stir things up.*

Regardless of how many times you ask and answer the same question, treat every instance as if it is the first time. *Always act on your answer—do or fulfill it.* Then ask and answer the question again. Every time you answer the question will lead to a surge of energy in your performance and usually leads to new approaches to playing the action. There are many different approaches to almost any problem or objective and answering the question in the moment can lead to spontaneously discovering and fulfilling them, all while the camera is on you. The spontaneity ensures the editor will stay on you as you nail the close-up.

Solution #5 — Doublethink

As you say your lines, think about something that is the opposite of what you are saying. The effort will complicate your thinking and show on your face as a thoughtfulness that adds a little mystery to what you are saying and thinking. The editor will stay on you because the audience will want to solve the mystery. This approach was used extensively by Robert De Niro when he played the lead in *The Last Tycoon* and had to portray the successful head of a movie studio who had a superior mind to those around him.

Solution #6 — Pre-Scene

If the close-up shot is in the middle of a scene, while waiting for "Action" to be called, run the scene with your scene partner up to the "Action" cue so you are firing on all cylinders. If the close-up shot is at the beginning of a scene, engage your scene partner, if he is willing, to improvise with you what's happening and spoken up to the moment of "Action." This might be called a Pre-Scene Improv [p. 229].

Solution #7 — Review Your Choices

Remind yourself what your choices are for: (1) what you want, need, or desire at this moment in the scene (the *problem*). (2) what the *obstacle(s)* are to you getting that. (3) what you are doing—your chosen verb (the *action*)—to overcome your obstacle(s) and get you what you want (seduce him, impress her, warn them). Focus on these choices while preparing for "Action" to be called and during the shot, especially the doing of the verb choice. If the other characters speak while the camera is on your close-up, make sure you hear their dialogue and integrate your response to it with the doing of your verb choice. Be open to the possibility of spontaneously changing what you are doing due to something you hear or how it is said to you. Follow your impulses.

CAREER

There is absolutely no substitute for genuine lack of preparation.
—Mike Nichols

Sooner or later we all sit down to a banquet of consequences.
—Robert Louis Stevenson

WHEN YOU NEED TO

IMPROVE YOUR SELF-TAPES

If you know how to prepare a self-tape audition, including knowing the material, creating the character, and showing how you might approach the role or what *you* can bring to it (that is, having a point of view about the scene), yet your self-tapes have minimal success, here are two solutions that address issues you may not have been mindful about.

Solution #1 — Listening

What you are doing while the other characters speak needs to be as interesting, if not more so, than what you are doing when you have the lines. Look at what you are doing when the other characters have lines. In the real production, the editor may cut away from your character while the others are speaking. In a self-tape audition, it's a one-person show. Just standing there being a good listener is not competitive with the other actors auditioning because you are not using all of your screen time to impress with your acting. When the other characters speak, take the opportunity to portray your character's inner life. Keep making and playing choices and keep acting while others speak. What kind of choices? That depends on your personal acting technique. The choices might include:

▶ Focus on your objective. What do you want in the scene, and how might that be affected by what others are saying? Does what you hear affect your strategy for achieving your objective?

▶ While the others speak, without anticipating your own next lines, start your acting choice for your next lines and let the others' lines support, thwart, or influence that choice in some way.

▶ While listening to the other's lines, select a moment (a turning point) to use as a cue to make the transition to your next acting choice for when you speak again—an action, emotion, conflict, agreement, or story point response. Make the transition at a turning point in the others' lines—either preselected or improvised in the moment. When you get your cue to speak, you will already be playing your acting choice.

▶ Play your subtext.

▶ Use what you are hearing to propel you further along an emotion arc [see Intensify an Emotion Instead of Flatlining, p. 147, and Emotion Arc, p. 51].

▶ Pursue Question and Answer Railroad Tracks [p. 3].

▶ React nonverbally, with your character's personality, to what you are hearing. For example, your reaction might express the thought "I can't believe what you're saying" or "That's so true." Any physicalized response showing how you think or feel about what you are hearing might portray the character's inner life. Keep it small.

▶ A simple activity can be added to all of the above choices—for example, put tobacco in a pipe, adjust your makeup, fold laundry. The activity should be appropriate for the character.

Regardless of your choice, what you do while others speak should connect you to what you do when you speak next. When the other characters have lines, make and play choices that are specific, not generic.

Solution #2 — Slating

Slating—saying your name and height—is done for identification purposes in the casting process. It replaces a picture and resume accompanying a live audition. While not seeming to, in its own way, it also replaces any chitchat that usually occurs before or after a live audition.

If your slate is at the beginning of your self-tape, it will be your first exposure to the casting people, which means it will influence their evaluation. Approach the slating in the same way you would handle arriving (in the room) at a live audition. Choose one of these approaches: (1) Slate in character. (2) Slate as yourself and then show them your acting ability by transforming into the role for the audition. (3) Slate as yourself at the character's energy level, which increases the casting director's receptivity to you as the character without typecasting you for future roles. (You will still get to show them your acting ability by completing the transformation into the character for the audition.) (4) Slate with energy that is the polar opposite of the character's energy at the end of the audition material. For example, if the character ends the audition with positive energy, slate with negative or neutral energy.

If your slate is at the end of your self-tape or in a separate file, the above four approaches are still applicable. In addition, if you choose either #1 or #3, you have an opportunity to briefly enhance the audition with something they weren't expecting. Besides saying your name and height in character, you can then complete the slate with a physical gesture, such as a tip of the hat, a salute, or a wink. Keep it in character and extremely simple. Think of it as a silent tag or button that tops off the audition, helping the casting people remember your characterization and, at the same time, providing a tease for the inventiveness they will get if they cast you. If you add a physical gesture, make sure it works. Don't do it just for the sake of doing something. How do you know if it works? If a viewer (you, a friend, or your agent or manager) smiles, you are good to go.

Different auditions require different approaches. You get to choose what works best for you for each audition. With self-tapes, unlike live auditions, you get to try all four approaches before deciding which one works best. Whichever you choose to do, choose it! Don't throw away your on-camera slating time with an unintentional approach. It's the beginning or end of your audition—use it! If you have always slated with the same approach and are not pleased with your self-tape results, trying a different approach can't hurt.

More Do's and Don'ts for Improving Your Self-Tapes

Don't be nervous when slating. Be relaxed, comfortable, and confident. Don't add extra material to the slate. Casting people hate it when you add more than what is required. You would be surprised how many actors add little or big monologues about why they would be perfect for the part. Instead of telling them, show them with your audition.

Should you use an accent for your audition, also use it for the slate. If your self-tape is successful and you go further in the casting process (such as a live callback), use the accent for the audition part of the callback, but drop the accent when schmoozing with the casting people. That's the time to show them you are taking on an accent for the character.

Make sure your performance fulfills the character description in the breakdown. If it doesn't, there has to be a strong and relevant reason for the direction or point of view you are taking based on your own interpretation.

Keep your self-tapes on your phone. You never know when you will need them. For example, you might show up to shoot, and the director will have you try multiple ways to approach the character and the scene. Finally, he'll say, "Just do what you did in the audition." A quick peek at your phone and you're ready to go.

WHEN YOU NEED TO

ACCEPT OR REJECT A JOB

If you have doubts about accepting a role, organizing your thoughts and feelings about it can be helpful.

Solution

Veteran actors talk about three criteria for taking a job:

(1) You want the paycheck.

(2) It will further your career.

(3) It will teach you something new and important as an actor.

If two out of the three criteria are met, why not do it?

Things to consider when looking at whether it can teach you something good as an actor are: Will it stretch you as an actor? Is there something you can learn from it? Does it require parts of your personality you have not shown? Does it require character traits you have never previously attempted? Are you a little scared of doing it? Do you want to work with the director or someone in the cast? When Jason Alexander considers taking a stage role, he asks himself: "Is the thing you're asking me to do, something that I don't know how to do when I start? That interests me more."

WHEN YOU NEED TO

INCREASE YOUR OPPORTUNITIES

Seeking employment may not be fun, and when your ego tells you, "You're better than this," let your id respond, "Not today. Deal with it." Winston Churchill told us that "Success is the ability to go from one failure to another with no loss of enthusiasm."

If you would like to increase your career opportunities, including new representation, auditions, and participation in project workshops, introduce this exercise into your daily life.

Solution

Instead of waiting for a text, email, or the phone to ring—which is a victim stance—initiate three business communications a day, Monday through Friday. Do this and your career opportunities will rise at an exponential rate.

Treat it like a game in which you will have to figure out whom to reach out to and what to say. Of course, you must continue with everything you are already doing to advance your career, such as sending out pictures, résumés, video reels; following up on agent and manager leads; going to open calls; attending an experiential class in which you work in every class; and keeping your presence on casting websites —Actors Access, Casting Network, *Backstage*, and Casting Frontier—updated. Starting today—or tomorrow at the latest—make three extra communications a day for business. By the time you have reached out to fifty new contacts, one of them may lead to something.

You might send an email to an agent whom a friend talked about. Perhaps you could call a theater director you met at a party. This exercise will force you to be creative and diligent in extending your career. If you do this exercise for just one week, you will have created energy in fifteen new areas. After a year, 750! Put that much more energy out there and you will see a return on your investment. And while you are doing this exercise you will, at least, feel much better about yourself and your career because you are being proactive instead of feeling helpless.

Rick Pagano, a casting director for film, TV, and theater (*Hotel Rwanda*, *X-Men*, *24*, *Proof*) advises, "If I were an actor, I would call all the casting directors who are in the book. Ten of them may get angry. The ones who pick up their phones and talk to you are the ones you want to do business with anyway. You'd be amazed at how many people actually *do* take your phone calls, and how many people *do* want your picture and résumé. Think of yourself as a salesman. They go and knock at a hundred doors and ninety-five will say no, but five might say yes. Most of the time, when you call a casting office, you might end up talking with an assistant. But remember, in this business, this year's assistant is maybe next year's casting director. Be your own cheerleader, your own inspirer, and your own secretary. Call people and try to meet every agent and casting director. If we, the casting community, don't know you exist, how are we going to hire you? Do take charge of your career. Don't be a victim. We need your uniqueness."

APPENDIX A — SAMPLE UMBRELLA ARCS

ABANDONMENT #1
- angry
- scared
- lonely

ABANDONMENT #2
- hurt
- loss
- fear
- sorrow
- anger

ABANDONMENT #3
- nervous
- embarrassed
- frustrated
- needy
- hurt
- bitter
- betrayed
- anger
- despair

ANGER
- fear
- sadness
- hurt
- frustration
- irritation
- rage

APPRECIATION
- disdain
- accuse
- curious
- interested
- appreciative
- impressed
- proud

ASHAMED
- embarrassed
- defensive
- bitter
- ashamed
- lonely
- hopeless
- despair

AWE
- open
- curious
- attentive
- pleased
- impressed
- amazed
- inspired
- awe
- stupefied
- transcendent

BACK FROM DEFEAT
- defeated
- hopeful
- courageous
- happy
- defiant
- victory

BETRAYED #1
- aware
- suspicious
- frustrated
- resentful
- bitter
- anger/fury

BETRAYED #2
- bitter
- spiteful
- sarcasm
- vindictive
- hate
- punish

BETRAYED #3
- aware
- suspicious
- devious
- confrontational
- angry
- fury
- rage
- satisfied

BRAGGART
- smug
- cocky
- macho
- arrogant
- thrilled

CELEBRATING POWER
- false humility
- enjoy
- savor
- proud
- revel
- brag
- show off

CHALLENGING (TO BE GREAT)
- dismissive
- humility
- baiting
- enthusiasm
- challenging

COURAGE #1
- uncertain
- nervous
- calm
- hopeful
- assured
- confident
- arrogant

COURAGE #2
honest
hopeful
confident
determined
brave
bold

DESPAIR
nostalgic
lost
sad
bitter
miserable
hopeless

EVIL
teasing
hurtful
taunting
spiteful
malicious
cruel
vile
vicious

FACING DEATH
denial/isolation
anger
depression
bargaining
acceptance

GUILT
fear
anxious to be forgiven
sad
confusion
remorse
want to please
futility

COWARDLY / GUILTY
embarrassed
weak
ashamed
sad
depressed
scared
anger

DESTROYED
confused
embarrassed
sad
grief
despair

EXCITEMENT OF LEARNING
frustrated
curious
enthusiastic
satisfied
cynical

FEAR #1
aware
concerned
suspicious
nervous
alarmed
agitated
scared
frightened
terrified
horrified

HAPPY #1
calm
content
pleased
amused
gay/glad
cheerful
giddy
jubilant
happy
elated
joyous

DEFIANCE / REBELLION
oppressed
suffocated
anger
shrewd
outburst
freedom

ENCOURAGEMENT
hope
excited
humility
proud
love

EXCITEMENT OF TEACHING
disappointed
frustrated
searching
tempting
baiting
bribery
curious
enthusiasm
passion
excited
joy

FEAR #2
cautious
nervous
anxious
apprehensive

HAPPY #2
content
confident
amused
happy
joyous
euphoric

HAUNTED/TORMENTED #1
- aware
- wary
- suspicious
- nervous
- scared
- possessed
- terrified

HAUNTED/TORMENTED #2
- lonely
- wary/cautious
- suspicious
- apprehensive

HOPEFUL
- aware
- possibility
- risk
- longing

HURT
- defensive
- frustrated
- sarcastic
- angry

INUNDATION
- confusion
- frustration
- disappointed
- irritated
- suffocated
- fear

JEALOUS
- fear
- sad
- angry

LIFE FULFILLMENT
- content
- loving
- happy
- careless
- excited
- joyous
- ecstasy

LOSS
- hurt
- anger
- sorrow

LOSS OF ILLUSION #1
- anger
- snob/regal
- guilty/confession
- defensive
- despair

LOSS OF ILLUSION #2
- confused
- embarrassed
- sad
- grief
- despair

LOSS OF ILLUSION #3
- sad
- embarrassed
- confused
- grief

LOSS OF ILLUSION #4
- defensive
- guilty
- sad
- confused
- lonely
- lost
- despair

MANIC DEPRESSION OR BIPOLAR
- depressed
- euphoria
- irritated

ORGASMIC
- arousal
- stimulation
- pleasure
- tension
- release
- ecstasy

PASSION
- concern
- commitment
- desire
- inspire
- excitement

PREPARATION FOR HARD NEWS
- alert
- caution
- warn
- console
- nurture
- encourage
- inspire

RESENTMENT #1
- frustrated
- irritated
- sarcasm
- aggravated
- hatred
- bitter
- anger

RESENTMENT #2
- disbelief
- aggravated
- bitter

SADIST/TORTURER
- resentment
- bitter
- hate
- punish
- anger/rage
- power
- satisfaction
- pleasure
- arousal

SEDUCTION
- entice
- lure
- tempt
- delight
- bribe

SELF-PITY #1
- resentment
- lonely/sad
- fear/terror
- confused

SELF-PITY #2
- lonely
- rejected
- resentment
- confused
- fear
- anger
- terror
- hysteria

SOLICITOUS
- attentive
- caring
- concerned
- anxious (desire)
- eager
- apprehensive
- troubled

STRENGTH
- brave
- proud
- determined
- humility

SUPPORT
- helpful
- supportive
- correcting
- helpful
- commiserating

APPENDIX B — SAMPLE CHARACTER ARCS

Painful	→	Joyful
Anger	→	Affection
Sadness	→	Joy
Hate	→	Love
Loneliness	→	Community
Hurt	→	Relief
Boredom	→	Involvement
Frustration	→	Contentment
Inferiority	→	Equality
Suspicion	→	Trust
Repulsion	→	Attraction
Shyness	→	Curiosity
Confusion	→	Clarity
Unfulfillment	→	Satisfaction
Weakness	→	Strength
Guilt	→	Innocence
Shame	→	Pride
Emptiness	→	Contentment
Emptiness	→	Fulfillment

APPENDIX C — SAMPLE EMOTION AND ATTITUDE CHOICES

STRONG		WEAK		HAPPY	FEAR
able	loud	apologetic	stale	admire	afraid
active	love	awkward	submissive	aglow	aghast
adequate	mean	confused	subtle	alive	alarmed
aggressive	mighty	considering	timid	amused	amazed
angry	mischievous	cynical	unable	anxious	anxious
arrogant	muscular	deathly	unconvincing	blissful	appalled
assured	nurturing	defeated	undernourished	bubbly	apprehensive
authoritative	opinionated	defective	unfit	calm	awed
bold	overwhelming	defenseless	unhinged	cheerful	cautious
brave	positive	deficient	unstable	compassion	chicken
capable	potent	deflated	useless	content	concerned
challenging	powerful	delicate	vulnerable	delighted	confused
cocky	probing	disabled	wavering	demure	considering
cold	productive	dismissive	wishy-washy	ecstatic	curious
compassion	quick	dull	wobbly	elated	daunted
confident	rage	exhausted	worn out	enthralled	displeasure
considering	reliable	exposed		enthusiastic	distrustful
consistent	resistant	feeble		excited	dreadful
correcting	resolute	fragile		exuberant	fearful
courageous	respectful	frail		feel good	foreboding
cynical	reverential	frustrated		felicitous	frightened
determined	robust	gentle		fine	harassed
dismissive	secure	helpless		fortunate	horrified
durable	snob	hopeful		full of life	incredulous
efficient	solid	humble		gay	insecure
enduring	stalwart	humility		gentle	intimidated
energetic	staunch	ill		giddy	jumpy
enthusiasm	stout	impotent		glad	leery
everlasting	suave	inadequate		gleeful	lonely
excited	super	incapable		good	meek
fierce	supportive	inconsistent		grateful	nervous
firm	surviving	ineffective		great	overwhelmed
forceful	testing	inferior		happy	panicky
formal	victorious	insecure		joyful	panic-stricken
formidable	violent	irresolute		joyous	petrified
forthright	warn	lacking		jubilant	puzzled
frank	well-being	languid		lighthearted	rattled
full of spirit	zealous	lethargic		love	shaky
generous		lifeless		lucky	shy
gentle		lost		marvelous	spooked
glorious		meager		memorable	startled
hale		mild		merry	stunned
hardy		pale		mischievous	suspicious
hate		passive		motherly	terrified
healthy		powerless		overjoyed	terrorized
helpful		probing		peaceful	threatened
herculean		puny		pleasant	timid
hopeful		quiet		proud	timorous
humble		retiring		relieved	tormented
humility		run-down		satisfied	tremulous
independent		shaky		smiley	uneasy
indestructible		shy		thankful	unpleasant
intense		sickly		thrilled	unstrung
invincible		soft		tranquil	unsure
interrogate		spineless		turned on	wary
knowing		squeamish		up	worried
				uplifted	
				wonderful	

ANGRY

aggravated	outraged
agitated	patronizing
anguished	perturbed
annoyed	provoked
apoplectic	punishing
arrogant	rage
bitter	raving
blustery	revengeful
bothered	riled
burned up	sarcastic
cold	seething
correcting	smug
critical	sneering
cross	snob
cutting	sore
cynical	spiteful
defensive	stormy
denigrating	temper
disgruntled	tense
disgusted	threat
dismayed	troubled
dismissive	uncontrollable
displeased	unrestrained
distraught	warn
distressed	
disturbed	
efficient	
enraged	
exasperated	
fed up	
fierce	
fiery	
frantic	
frenzied	
frustrated	
furious	
hateful	
hostile	
hot-tempered	
in a stew	
incensed	
indignant	
inflamed	
infuriated	
intense	
irate	
irked	
irritated	
livid	
mad	
madness	
mean	
miffed	
minimizing	
offended	
outburst	

SAD

angry	sober
apathetic	somber
bad	sorrowful
blue	sorry
burdened	terrible
cynical	turned off
crushed	uneasy
defeated	unhappy
deflated	unloved
dejected	unpleasant
despairing	unwanted
desperate	upset
despondent	vulnerable
depressed	
disappointed	
disenchanted	
disillusioned	
distressed	
disturbed	
down	
downcast	
downhearted	
downtrodden	
drab	
dreary	
dull	
emotional	
failure	
feel unwanted	
foreboding	
forlorn	
gloomy	
glum	
grave	
grieved	
hate	
heavy-hearted	
hopeless	
hurt	
lonely	
lost	
low	
low spirits	
melancholy	
miserable	
mistrustful	
moody	
morose	
mournful	
negative	
painful	
pitiful	
plaintive	
remorseful	
sad	
self-pitying	

CONFUSED

abashed
amazed
anxious
astounded
baffled
befuddled
bewildered
bothered
chaotic
confounded
confused
crazy
dazed
depressed
deranged
disconcerted
dismayed
disordered
disorganized
disoriented
distracted
distraught
disturbed
doubtful
dubious
embarrassed
flabbergasted
flustered
foggy
forgetful
frustrated
helpless
hopeless
incredulous
mistaken
misunderstood
mixed up
muddled
obscure
out of it
panicky
perplexed
probing
puzzled
scatterbrained
surprised
trapped
troubled
uncertain
uncomfortable
undecided
unsettled
unsure
upset
vague
weak

LOVE

affection
desire
erotic
exotic
excited
favor
flirtatious
horny
intimate
kind
longing
lovelorn
loving
orgasmic
passion
release
respect
seductive
sexy
stimulated
tender
tension
willing

APPENDIX D — SAMPLE ATTITUDE LINES

I can do it.
I can't.
I don't get it.
I hate men.
I hate women.
I hate you.
I have to.
I hurt.
I know best.
I know better.
I know it all.
I love everybody.
I love men.
I love women.
I love you.
I need it.
I want help.
I want it.
I want more.
I want out.
I'll help.
I'm a con.
I'm a screw-up.
I'm a rebel.
I'm a winner.
I'm a wreck.
I'm abrupt.
I'm adventurous.
I'm afraid.
I'm aghast.
I'm agile.
I'm alive!
I'm alone.
I'm amazing.
I'm ambitious.
I'm analytical.
I'm anxious.
I'm aristocratic.
I'm awkward.
I'm bitter.
I'm bored.

I'm boring.
I'm bossy.
I'm broken.
I'm careless.
I'm caring.
I'm casual.
I'm certain.
I'm chaotic.
I'm charitable.
I'm chatty.
I'm clever.
I'm cold.
I'm combative.
I'm concerned.
I'm confident.
I'm cool.
I'm crazed.
I'm cunning.
I'm cynical.
I'm dangerous.
I'm daring.
I'm decent.
I'm defensive.
I'm defiant.
I'm definite.
I'm demanding.
I'm depressed.
I'm desperate.
I'm detailed.
I'm determined.
I'm devoted.
I'm direct.
I'm disgusted.
I'm distracted.
I'm distrusting.
I'm dogged.
I'm driven.
I'm eager.
I'm earnest.
I'm easy.
I'm educated.

I'm efficient.
I'm egotistical.
I'm elegant.
I'm enthusiastic.
I'm exotic.
I'm fair.
I'm fancy.
I'm fast.
I'm fastidious.
I'm fearful.
I'm feeble.
I'm fervent.
I'm fickle.
I'm flashy.
I'm flexible.
I'm forceful.
I'm forgiving.
I'm fragile.
I'm frank.
I'm free.
I'm fresh.
I'm fun.
I'm funny.
I'm furtive.
I'm generous.
I'm gorgeous.
I'm grasping.
I'm growing.
I'm happy.
I'm headstrong.
I'm healing.
I'm honest.
I'm horny.
I'm hot.
I'm hungry.
I'm impatient.
I'm important.
I'm in charge.
I'm in control.
I'm industrious.
I'm insistent.

I'm kind.
I'm knowledgeable.
I'm lasting.
I'm lazy.
I'm limp.
I'm lively.
I'm logical.
I'm lonely.
I'm loud.
I'm loving.
I'm lucky.
I'm malicious.
I'm manipulative.
I'm messy.
I'm meticulous.
I'm moral.
I'm nervous.
I'm neurotic.
I'm nimble.
I'm noble.
I'm nothing.
I'm old.
I'm open.
I'm opinionated.
I'm organized.
I'm outgoing.
I'm parental.
I'm passionate.
I'm patient.
I'm perceptive.
I'm perky.
I'm perplexed.
I'm phony.
I'm plain.
I'm playful.
I'm pleasant.
I'm pleased.
I'm plodding.
I'm political.
I'm powerful.
I'm pragmatic.
I'm precious.
I'm precise.

I'm prejudiced.
I'm punctual.
I'm pushy.
I'm reasonable.
I'm refined.
I'm relentless.
I'm religious.
I'm resistant.
I'm respectable.
I'm romantic.
I'm rustic.
I'm sassy.
I'm satisfied.
I'm scared.
I'm scrutinizing.
I'm searching.
I'm seasick.
I'm secretive.
I'm selfless.
I'm sensible.
I'm sentimental.
I'm sexy.
I'm shocked.
I'm shrewd.
I'm sincere.
I'm skittish.
I'm slick.
I'm smart.
I'm smarter.
I'm sneaky.
I'm snide.
I'm snotty.
I'm sorry.
I'm spirited.
I'm stern.
I'm stoned.
I'm stubborn.
I'm stuffy.
I'm stupid.
I'm stylish.
I'm superior.
I'm suspicious.
I'm sweet.

I'm the best.
I'm the king.
I'm thoughtful.
I'm thrifty.
I'm tired.
I'm tough.
I'm turned on.
I'm unbridled.
I'm uncompromising.
I'm unconscious.
I'm unpretentious.
I'm unruffled.
I'm unyielding.
I'm upright.
I'm vexing.
I'm visionary.
I'm warm.
I'm willing.
I'm winning.
I'm wise.
I'm witty.
I'm worried.
I'm worth it.
I'm worthless.
I need meaning.
I used to be king.
It's okay.
Keep it neat.
Leave me alone.
Let's party!
Life sucks.
Life's a party!
Look at me!
Love me.
Nobody loves me.
Party down!
Please!
Stay away.
We're all brothers!
Why me?

APPENDIX E — SAMPLE ACTION (VERBS) CHOICES

Note: An excellent resource for selecting active verbs is *Actions: The Actors' Thesaurus* by Marina Caldarone and Maggie Lloyd-Williams (Drama Publishers).

abolish	brag	crucify	entice
absolve	bribe	crush	entrap
abuse	brood	curse	eradicate
accuse	cajole	damn	erupt
admire	calculate	dare	escape
admonish	call	deceive	estimate
adore	catch	deduce	evade
affirm	caution	defy	evaluate
afflict	censure	delight	examine
aid	challenge	demand	excuse
allow	charm	demean	execute
amaze	chastise	denigrate	explode
amuse	cheat	deny	exploit
annoy	check	discourage	facilitate
antagonize	cheer	discredit	flatter
anticipate	chide	destroy	flaunt
apologize	clarify	detect	flirt
appeal	cloak	deter	frighten
applaud	coax	devastate	frustrate
approach	coddle	dictate	gag
arouse	coerce	direct	gauge
arrange	collude	discard	gladden
assess	command	discover	gloat
assist	commend	dismiss	goad
astound	con	distract	grieve
attack	conceal	divert	harangue
badger	concern	divine	hassle
baffle	conciliate	dodge	help
bait	condemn	dominate	henpeck
bask	condescend	dramatize	hide
beckon	confide	duck	hoodwink
beg	confirm	ease	humble
beguile	confound	educate	humiliate
belittle	confuse	elevate	humor
berate	consider	elicit	hurt
bestow	contest	elucidate	hush
bewitch	convince	embrace	hypnotize
bid	correct	enchant	idolize
blame	corroborate	endear	ignore
bless	court	engross	imitate
bluff	cover	enlighten	impair
boast	criticize	entertain	implicate

276

impress	organize	rave	strike
incite	overlook	read	strip
indict	panic	rebuke	strut
indoctrinate	patronize	rectify	suggest
induce	perform	reiterate	summon
indulge	perplex	reject	support
inflame	persecute	rejoin	suppress
insinuate	peruse	release	surprise
inspect	pester	relegate	surrender
inspire	placate	remedy	swindle
instruct	plan	renege	tantalize
insult	plead	repel	taunt
interview	please	repress	teach
invade	pledge	reprimand	tease
invite	ponder	repulse	tempt
judge	pontificate	rescue	terrify
lambast	pose	resist	test
lampoon	pounce	retract	thwart
lead	pray	retreat	tickle
lecture	preen	revolt	threaten
libel	preoccupy	ridicule	titillate
liberate	prepare	sanctify	tolerate
lure	prevail	satisfy	torment
malign	prick	savor	torture
maneuver	prod	scheme	trick
manipulate	primp	scold	tyrannize
marshall	probe	scrutinize	understand
mask	promise	search	uproot
mend	promote	sedate	urge
mimic	prompt	seduce	validate
mislead	propagandize	settle	verify
misuse	propel	shake	victimize
mobilize	propose	shame	vilify
mock	prosecute	shock	vindicate
mortify	protect	show off	ward off
mother	provoke	shroud	warn
motivate	purge	shun	welcome
mourn	purify	simplify	withdraw
muffle	pursue	slander	woo
muster	put down	smother	worship
mystify	quash	soothe	wrangle
notify	quench	spoil	yearn
nullify	query	squash	
obliterate	question	squelch	
offend	rally	stalk	
ogle	ratify	startle	
oppose	ravage	stretch	

ACKNOWLEDGMENTS

To preserve my sanity during the COVID lockdown I hunkered down and wrote *Secret Magic Stuff for Actors*. The original idea for the book came from meeting with a Zoom group of actor friends and former students discussing the need for a reference book where you could look up how to do this or that. The first thank-yous go to that group for participating in the idea's inception and following up by reading and commenting on parts of early drafts: Anna Khaja, Nardeep Khurmi, and Sachin Bhatt. Very special thanks to Sharon Carnicke for her incisive reading and extended commentary on the first draft. I also thank my former students who brought their considerable insight to reading parts of early drafts and providing helpful feedback: Kurtwood Smith, Elizabeth Dement, Rob Welsh, Joy Nash, Michelle McGregor, Meredith Riley Stewart, Stacie Greenwell, Samantha Valdellon, Scott Krinsky, Jeff Sugarman, Victor Anthony, and my workshop assistants Kevin Ashworth and Marissa Ingrasci. And hugs and thanks to friends for their valuable comments: Leo Braudy, Miguel Arteta, Justine Arteta, Melissa Manchester, Reba Thomas, Jason Kravits, Mathew Jaeger, Tania Vega, and Jennifer Gouchoe. Immense gratitude goes to Darlene Basche for vetting the psychology material and her overall support. A big thank-you to the publisher, Gwen Feldman at Silman-James Press, for her great support in so many ways. Kudos to editor Mike Levine for all his help, especially in dealing with the organization of this book.

ABOUT THE AUTHOR

Stephen Book is an acting teacher, coach, and director best known for creating Improvisation Technique: improvisational acting applied to scripted performances for film, stage, and television. In 1985 he opened the Stephen Book Acting Workshop in Hollywood, now in its 39th year.

His students have included Academy Award winners William Hurt, Rita Moreno, and Robin Williams, as well as Val Kilmer, Maura Tierney, Sanaa Lathan, Carla Gugino, Tim Matheson, Valerie Mahaffey, Malcolm Jamal-Warner, David Boreanaz, Tate Donovan, Janis Paige, Larry Drake, Kurtwood Smith, William Schallert, Grant Heslov, and stand-up comics George Carlin, Adam Ferrara, and Christopher Titus.

Stephen has also coached singers for roles in film and TV including Randy Travis, Michael Hutchence (INXS), Mindy McCready, and Ozzie Osbourne. He was creative consultant to Melissa Manchester on her Grammy-nominated "Don't Cry Out Loud" and to the director Vincent Ward on the Oscar winning film *What Dreams May Come*, starring Robin Williams.

ABOUT THE AUTHOR

As an undergraduate at Sarah Lawrence College, Stephen studied with the legendary Viola Spolin. They later co-designed the Spolin Theater Game Center in Hollywood, where he served as executive director and principal teacher. He received an MFA in directing at Stanford University and studied with Lee Strasberg in the Directors Unit at the Actors Studio.

At the age of twenty-eight, he joined the faculty of The Juilliard School (1973-1981). He has also taught at Stanford, Brown, Bread Loaf School of English, USC (1977-1991), UCLA, the Esalen Institute, Circle in the Square Theater School, in London at the Globe Shakespeare Center, and in Moscow at both the Russian state theater school (GITIS) and as keynote speaker at the international conference on Modern Methods of the Actor's Psychotechnique at the Stanislavsky Center.

He has directed productions Off Broadway and in regional and university theaters, including Washington Theater Club, Los Angeles Actors Theater, Stanford Repertory Theater, Equity Library Theatre, New Dramatists, Princeton, Brown, Sarah Lawrence, USC, and the Theater of Dionysus in Athens.

His books include *Book on Acting: Improvisation Technique for the Professional Actor in Film, Theater and Television* (also translated and published in Poland) and *The Actor Takes a Meeting*.

Also published by **Silman-James Press**
Available wherever books are sold.

"Stephen Book manages to articulate a technique that both allows the actor to be specific in silence and active and emotionally affective when speaking. He helps you tap into that endless well which is human."
—**Viola Davis**

"Improvisation is essential to acting and Book is a terrific teacher."
—**William Hurt**

"In adapting improvisation exercises to script work, Stephen Book challenges some of the received wisdom of modern American training and offers a practical method for professional actors who want to learn how to infuse their work with spontaneity. Book's exercises demonstrate how much further you can go, imaginatively speaking, when acting."
—*Backstage*

The ability to improvise a skilled performance while speaking scripted lines is of paramount importance to actors working in an industry which often allows very little rehearsal time. Through his innovative Improvisation Technique, Book shows the actor how to create a spontaneous performance by applying improvisation to traditional script-acting for film, theater, and television.

Book On Acting begins with training in how to improvise. Book's fundamental principle of improvisation is "Acting is doing, and there is always more to do." The actor learns what to do to keep himself in a spontaneous improvisational state while serving the purpose of the scene.

Book's Improvisation Technique is then applied to exercises with scripted lines, developing sophisticated improvisation skills for enhancing character, emotions, conflict, and agreement, as well as improving the actor's audition process. Included is a unique process for breaking down scripted scenes into improvisation choices and examples of film and television scenes in which Book-coached actors, used his Improvisation Technique to create their performances.

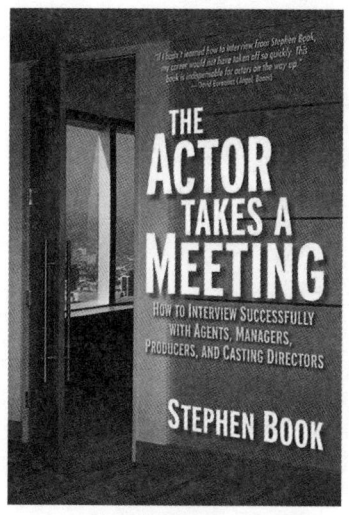

Actors must take meetings with agents, managers, producers, and casting directors to advance their careers. However, regardless of their acting abilities and credits these important meetings are often unsuccessful because the actors present themselves inadequately. Unknowingly, actors frequently conduct themselves as victims or manipulators, which leads to their being seen as undesirable working partners.

The Actor Takes A Meeting addresses the actor's self-presentation at an interview or meeting. It shows the actor how to be the host of a meeting and the initiator of an exciting experience that may lead to offers of representation, auditions, and project participation.

In *The Actor Takes a Meeting*, actors will learn startling, myth-busting truths: They'll learn that they will "blow it" if interviewers look at their résumés during meetings or if they answer questions with prepared riffs about themselves or if they are on their best behavior!

"Book so beautifully articulates the psychology behind the interview process that I heartily recommend his book to every actor I know—and to anyone else who interviews often but wonders why his or her success rate is so darn low."
—*Backstage*

"If I hadn't learned how to interview from Stephen Book, my career would not have taken off so quickly. This book is indispensable for actors on the way up."
—**David Boreanaz**

"Stephen Book's interview technique is one of the most valuable tools for the actor. It is a 'how-to' for making an authentic connection. I vividly remember one of the best general meetings I had—It was easy and fun, and the time just flew by. As we were saying goodbye and I finally glanced at her resume, I saw that she had indeed studied with Stephen Book. I was not surprised."
—**Liz Dean**, Casting Director (*The Good Doctor*, *Major Crimes*, *Star Trek: Picard*)

"The Actor Takes a Meeting is a guide to changing the actor's fear into authenticity and presence. This book is a gift to the actor."
—**April Webster**, Casting Director (*Criminal Minds*, *Lost*, *Star Trek*)